THE CONTENTED COUNTRYMAN

The Best of
C. Henry Warren

Edited by

Geoffrey R. Warren

Illustrated by

John Cackett

ALAN SUTTON

First published in the United Kingdom in 1991
Alan Sutton Publishing Ltd · Phoenix Mill · Far Thrupp · Stroud
Gloucestershire

First published in the United States of America in 1991
Alan Sutton Publishing Inc · Wolfeboro Falls · NH 03896-0848

British Library Cataloguing in Publication Data

The contented countryman : the best of C. Henry Warren.
1. England. Rural regions. Social life, history. Warren,
C. Henry (Clarence Henry) 1895–1966
I. Warren, Geoffrey 1951–
942.0858092

ISBN 0-86299-945-6

Library of Congress Cataloging in Publication Data applied for

Jacket illustration by
John Cackett

Typeset in Garamond 12/13.
Typesetting and origination by
Alan Sutton Publishing Limited.
**Printed and Bound in Great Britain by
Hartnolls Limited, Bodmin, Cornwall.**

Contents

CONTENTS

CONTENTS

Acknowledgements

My sources have been many, not least the large body of articles, letters and references that I traced in order to fill out impressions gleaned from fifty books which in one way or another carry the name of C. Henry Warren. (A list of his major works is located at the end of this anthology.) However I am supremely in the debt of John Gili and his wife Elizabeth (Henry's closest friends) who have been unstinting in their generosity and support for my efforts to research and promote my great-uncle's achievements. My initial visit to their home near Oxford was a particular joy as they shared their memories of Henry Warren and gave me access to valuable documentation. To them as well as to the firm of literary agents headed by Gerald Pollinger must go credit for helping to get three of C. Henry Warren's books back into print in the 1980s (*A Boy in Kent*, *A Cotswold Year* and *England is a Village*). It has been gratifying to witness the enthusiasm that a new generation of admirers has shown for the craftsmanship of his best prose essays. Some of the positive feedback we have received has come from those whom I have had the opportunity of contacting in my researches, who either knew Henry as a child or in his adult life, and their information and comments have been most informative. Adrian Bell (a fellow countryside writer) was someone I enjoyed visiting at his home in Suffolk just before his death. The late Dodie Smith, the highly successful children's writer, was a neighbour in Finchingfield and she wrote to me a delightful appreciation of Henry Warren as a companion on country walks and rides. I was in touch by letter with Richard Church's daughter in New Zealand (and this contact led me to a rich resource of letters between Henry Warren and Richard Church in the University of Texas which my brother David was able to follow up during a year he spent in the USA). The widow of Frank Kendon got in touch after the re-publication of *A Boy in Kent* and as a result we were able to exchange various letters and information. I also discovered that Henry had played the organ at Frank and Celia Kendon's wedding. People like the Kemps and Cheesemans in Mereworth were useful informants. Not least, my visit to Finchingfield to see my great-aunt Ethel provided me with a 'warts and all' picture of her brother-in-law which complemented the understandably more romantic views of associates and acquaintances. As I write, Ethel Warren is still alive and approaching her one hundredth birthday.

Sources

The text in this book is taken from the following published and unpublished works:

from *English Cottages and Farmhouses*, Hertfordshire Holidays; from *A Boy in Kent*, Father and Son, Five Acre Field, Through the Eyes of a Child, East End Invaders; from *Mereworth School Magazine*, Greetings to Mereworth School; from *Countryman into Poet* radio programme, Boy into Poet; from unpublished autobiography, A Quick Change Library, The Piano in the Front Room, The Church on the Hill, Sufficient Amends, No More a Soldier, 'Those who can't – teach', To Essex, Frank Kendon in Cambridge, Sir John Reith, Goodnight Vienna, Out and About, To Essex Again, Epilogue; from *Best Short Stories of 1925* and *Cobbler, Cobbler and Other Stories*, While 'Zekiel Ploughed; from *The Stricken Peasant and Other Poems*, The Stricken Peasant; from *The Countryman*, Two Country Parsons; from *Orchards of the Sun*, Arrival in Provence; from *A Cotswold Year*, The Countryside in Winter; from *Happy Countryman*, A Trayful of Cherries; from *England is a Village*, England, Mutz; from *Adam was a Ploughman*, Rural Wit; from *Content with What I Have*, The Librarian; from *Woman's Hour* BBC Radio programme, Up with the Lark; from *The Sketch*, Promise of Spring; from *The Times*, The 'Black Horses' at Plough; from *Tyrolean Journal*, Alpine Interlude; from *Good Housekeeping*, They've Started Harvesting; from *The Thorn Tree*, Rhyme for a Farmer.

Introduction

─────

I met my great-uncle only once. In 1960 we were in Essex for a family holiday and decided to take a trip out to the village of Finchingfield, near Braintree which is in the north-west of the county. On the off-chance of him being at home we called in at 'Timbers' where C. Henry Warren spent the last thirty or so years of his life. My abiding impression is of a tall, stooping figure bending to get under the cottage's low doorways, and of books everywhere. It was books bearing the name of Warren displayed under the television in my grandparents' bungalow in Worthing, Sussex, which had fascinated me as a child. Henry and his brother Herbert (my grandfather) had little in common but they did retain contact, particularly until their mother's death in 1942. As a result, a substantial collection of Henry Warren's books in signed first editions has been preserved within the family, which I inherited on my grandfather's death. This initial interest in a famous writer in the family has developed into a more mature appreciation of the work of C. Henry Warren. Not only did I seek to complete my own collection of his major published and unpublished writings (a task in which I was greatly assisted by Liz Anderton, an enthusiastic and very effective second-hand book searcher from Bridgnorth, Shropshire) but there began a quest to discover more about his life from those who knew him. This has been an abiding interest for over twenty years.

Clarence Henry Warren was born on 12 June 1895 in Mereworth near Maidstone in Kent. This hop-growing region in the Medway valley is right at the heart of the Weald, 'the Garden of England'. One aspect of my research into his background has been into his (and therefore my) family tree. It has given me a picture of the environment from which Henry Warren is descended on both sides of his family. On the paternal side he can be traced to Jeremiah Warren, a labourer, who was born in the late eighteenth century. Jeremiah's son James (born about 1830) married Sarah Pearce on 8 December 1851 at St James (Clerkenwell, London). (Her father John Pearce was a labourer too). James Warren was a shoemaker and it is likely that he moved out of London into the adjacent country districts of South Hertfordshire once he was sufficiently successful at his trade to be more independent. From his marriage came three sons, the eldest of whom was William Warren born on 2 May 1864 at Wormley near Hoddeston in Hertfordshire.

William's birth took place therefore thirteen years after his parents' marriage. This combined with the fact that Henry was not born until William was thirty-one meant that Henry's paternal grandparents were only known to him in their seventies. However he did spend holidays with them and they are described by him with real affection in *English Cottages and Farmhouses*. However he did spend holidays with them and they are described by him with real affection in *English Cottages and Farmhouses*. Henry Warren came to respect the true countryman and this is evident in his books. He portrays his grandparents as pious both in their loyalty to country ways and the Christian faith they espoused. He inherited much from his countryside background although it was in a very different sense that he became a countryman himself. Childhood in Mereworth coupled with life in Essex and the Cotswolds as an adult laid a foundation for his authentic country books, which are among the very best produced in English this century. What Henry never became was a literary man who would despise his humble origins.

Turning to the maternal side, Henry's father William married a woman from his own area. The family of Alice Adams were of some standing in the district around Cheshunt. Itinerant and independent shoemakers would have been quite happy to see their sons marry into families like the Adams, who were not rich but had their own land and could claim a continuity over several generations. When I researched the Adams family in the Hertford Record Office I discovered that Henry's mother was descended from James Adams, who was born in 1720. He was Henry's great-great-great-great-grandfather so at least five generations had farmed Hammond Street and the area around about. On both sides of the family Henry had the countryside in his blood. His parents were married at Holy Trinity (Kilburn, London) on 11 May 1885. After two sons were born to them (Frank in 1886 and Herbert, my grandfather, in 1887) the family moved to Mereworth in Kent where William took over the village stores and where Clarence Henry was born in 1895.

The narrative of *A Boy in Kent* suggests that this gap between Henry and his older brothers was quite significant. We get the impression of an only child. Henry took a dislike to his first name Clarence and once out of the childhood environment he used Henry as his Christian name and the style 'C. Henry' for his public life. His parents appear in *A Boy in Kent* and in various unpublished writings which follow on from it and link it to the main autobiography (which Henry provisionally called *Content with What I Have*, although this title was used for another book after his death). Some of this previously unpublished material is contained in this anthology. William ran a prosperous business and was active in Mereworth life, especially the Horticultural Society where his organizational abilities (if not his expertise) were valued. He inspired in his youngest son a very deep regard, whereas Henry seems to have felt more remote from his mother, Alice, who probably did not indulge her son's natural exuberance. She died in 1942 fifteen years after her husband who drowned in a watercress bed in 1927. My father was born in Mereworth in 1920 but the family left the area soon afterwards and, as far as I have been able to determine, Henry never went back. When I visited the village in the late 1970s there were some who still remembered the family and the impact which *A Boy in Kent* had made on its first publication. Its author's fame is celebrated in the name of a cottage in the street next door to the village stores. Owing to necessary reroofing the owners renamed it 'Fladmere Cottage' after the fictional name Henry gave Mereworth in his book.

After attending the village school Henry went on to Maidstone Grammar School and from there he won a place at Goldsmiths College (University of London). His formal education was augmented by private music lessons at home and school. He not only played well enough for it to be considered at one time that he would have a musical career but he also deputized at the organ of Mereworth Parish

Church. At this time he was particularly influenced by the priest in charge at nearby East Peckham Church (Canon Ryley) whose superb musicianship attracted many people to his services at the isolated 'Church on the Hill'. The record of this now redundant church's history has been written by Margaret Lawrence. Canon Ryley was an acquaintance of Edward Elgar and a minor composer of church music in his own right. For a village boy, Henry was somewhat unexpectedly interested in the so-called new music of the pre-war period and even attempted to write his own pieces in their avant-garde style. Henry's parents always tried to take a pride in their son's flowering musicianship but his love of the less traditional type of music must have been hard for them to understand. Some evidence of his efforts is to be found in manuscripts which have come into my possession. Henry was acquainted with a young woman called Dorothy Lee with whom he entered piano duet competitions. She was to become a relative of the family when her cousin Ruby Johnson married Herbert (Henry's brother and my grandfather). Before her death she gave me one or two of these compositions which were dedicated to her.

It was possible for Henry Warren to glean something of value towards his cultural development in the rather isolated world of Mereworth but, although his parents never discouraged him, he lacked the companionship which would have assisted the process of growth. Instead he fed off the catholic diet of magazines which each week arrived at the stores and which he had the freedom to browse through before their rightful owners collected them. The lack of the classics in his own parents' library was for Henry not altogether a disadvantage for it allowed him to make his own selections from a far broader range. He decided to avoid a career in music because he had a fear of ending up like his own music teachers who were poorly paid and generally unappreciated for all their dedication. His alternative choice was teaching but this was entered without enthusiasm and Henry was fond of quoting the adage of George Bernard Shaw that 'those who can, do' but 'those who can't, teach'. Henry had scarcely completed his time of teacher training at Goldsmiths than he was called up to fight in the Middle East in the Royal Army Ordnance Corps with which he saw service in Egypt and Palestine. At this time he forged a deep friendship with the poet and critic Frank Kendon who, like Henry, was a product of the Kent countryside and who wrote his account of a Kentish childhood in *The Small Years*. They met at an embarkation camp, waiting to join a troopship for Egypt. The war years resulted in Henry's first published book, which was some trench poetry called *Pipes of Pan* and which constituted part of a great flood of such creativity that the terrible conflict seemed to inspire. The return to Mereworth in 1919 was unusually liberating for Henry in that it coincided with a glorious English springtime. He found the end of soldiering an enormous relief.

In the early 1920s Henry had teaching posts first at a Council School in Bromley (Kent) and then as English Master at Newport Grammar School in Essex. Going to Essex was to be a most significant move for him and with a few breaks he lived in the county for the rest of his life. This period was significant for the friendships he forged with the poet Percy Ripley and the artist/illustrator Alexander Walker. Henry greatly admired the work of Edmund Blunden and Richard Church, who were just then emerging as significant literary figures, and he developed lasting friendships with them also. In 1922 he made a break with paid employment and launched off on his own into freelance writing. Using a cottage in the Essex village of Widdington as his base he began to earn his living by the pen. Over the next six years with the assistance of some temporary jobs to eke out his finances he managed to survive. There were plenty of periodicals in which to get poems and prose pieces published and opportunities to review for magazines were coming to Henry as a result of his own growing reputation as a writer. In the 1920s there was a sequence of books which included *Wild Goose Chase* (the record of an abortive attempt to emigrate to Canada), *Cobbler, Cobbler and Other Stories* (in which he showed a very impressive range of skills in short story writing, sketches and non-fiction pieces) plus two volumes of his own poetry *The Stricken Peasant and Other Poems* and *The Secret Meadow and Other Poems* (some poems were included in both collections). He also edited an anthology of poetry for secondary school boys which brought him a steady income for most of the inter-war years. This was entitled *A Book of Verse for Boys*. His temporary jobs included a spell as assistant to H.N. Brailsford at *The New Leader* and the post of lecturer at the National Portrait Gallery in London.

However, from 1928 to 1932 C. Henry Warren went back into more reliable employment with the newly-formed BBC as a press officer in Manchester to begin with (where he gained valuable experience as an announcer) and then as Assistant Editor of *The Radio Times* under Eric Maschwitz. Eric was better known as Holt Marvell who with George Posford wrote 'Goodnight Vienna' and other romantic songs. It was with the musical side of broadcasting that Henry was mainly concerned and it gave him an opportunity to indulge his life-long love of both traditional and innovative music. He met and became a close friend of the composer Alan Rawsthorne and the Mozart expert Harry Blech. More exciting still were opportunities to meet the internationally-known composers Stravinsky and Delius. The result of his work on *The Radio Times* was the editorship of *The Men Behind the Music*, in which he gathered together his own essays on Handel and Mussorgsky plus contributions by H.N. Brailsford, Richard Church and Winifred Holtby. In the 1930s debate raged over the extent to which the BBC should serve up music for the masses and thereby offend the purists. W.J. Turner was one of those who agreed with Henry Warren's view that everyone should have access to the cultural life of our civilization and they not only became allies in the correspondence pages of the press but friends as well. Others on the fringes of Bloomsbury with whom Henry became friendly were Anthony Bertram (whom he had deputized for at the National Portrait Gallery), Hermon Ould (of PEN fame) and the actress Hermione Gingold (Eric Maschwitz's wife). Review work with *The Spectator* brought him in touch with the Stracheys and J.B. Priestley.

Henry's closer friendships included that with John Gili whom he met in Barcelona in the 1930s as the result of an article in *The Bookman*. Together with John's wife, Elizabeth, their circle included Helen Gaskell who was a constant friend and patron to Henry. Various holidays abroad were one luxury Henry enjoyed, visiting Luxembourg, Germany, Austria and Catalonia, but times of relaxation abroad never compensated for the inner frustration of these years in the later 1920s and early 1930s. Sir John Reith had warned Henry at his interview that the BBC expected him to give himself to it body and soul and this was a restrictiveness which became intolerable as his time with the Corporation went by. It led to a second breaking away which was to be more final. With the contacts he had made and experience gained, there were plenty of opportunities for Henry Warren to make a decent living at what he most enjoyed. This was the time when his career as a writer was set to flourish. Another holiday in the inter-war years had been to Provence and this was to be the inspiration for his first novel (*Orchards of the Sun*) published by Lovat Dickson. Nelson Novels published a second novel entitled *Beside Still Waters*, selected by L.A.G. Strong, and which owed much more to the rural life Henry had experienced as a child. There followed commissions for two guides (*The Writer's Art* and *Wise Reading*); of more substance was *Sir Philip Sidney: A Study in Conflict* which has remained in print in the USA right up to the present and which inspired Richard Church's poem 'Sidney's Love'. This entry into the field of serious biography marked Henry's growing maturity and self-confidence as a writer.

The most significant fruit of the BBC years was to come a little later. His experience of radio got him a commission to do some broadcasts about the Cotswolds, where he had gone to live in 1932 after leaving the Corporation. This regular series, which lasted for several years, gave birth to the book *A Cotswold Year*, a record of a year's life as seen from the window of 'Allanhay', his cottage in the village of Stockend near Edge in Gloucestershire. When I visited its present owners recently we were able to talk about Henry Warren's association with the area (where he is still remembered by the older folk) and admire the quite breathtaking view over the Severn to Wales. This initial work with BBC Radio led to numerous opportunities in broadcasting right up to the 1960s, and his voice became well known and loved 'on the wireless'. The *Out and About* series, as these Cotswold talks were called, immediately preceded the publication of *A Boy in Kent*. The significance of his physical move from city life back to the country lay in the inner journey he was making at this time back to childhood in Mereworth to rediscover his identity and core values.

By the mid-1930s and approaching forty, Henry was at the height of his powers. He largely abandoned poetry and in writing about country matters he found the genre that matched his abilities and background and in which he could achieve his finest work. His claim to be considered as a major exponent of the art of countryside writing rests largely on the Larkfield sequence of books written from and about the Essex village of Finchingfield. He moved here from the Cotswolds in the late 1930s, settling in a beautiful timbered cottage from where he wrote with deliberation and authority about the life of the corn belt of East Anglia. The series of books began with *Happy Countryman*, concerning Freddie Dare one of the village inhabitants. This was so popular that it appeared in a second edition a few years later. Then came *England is a Village*, which recorded the phoney war period in the early days of the Second World War when Essex was cut off from the world by huge snow drifts. There followed *The Land is Yours* and *Miles from Anywhere* which were more mixed collections of essays, and after the war Henry published *The Scythe in the Apple Tree*, which deals with his own house and its surroundings, and *Adam was a Ploughman*, the most humorous of the set. These books were varied in subject matter, sensitive in their descriptions of the natural and man-made landscape and informed by a profound and wide-ranging knowledge of everything agricultural. The theme of change in the farming communities he knew so well is something Henry tackled particularly well without idealizing the past and yet with a sense of rural life's continuity and abiding values. This outstanding vein of creativity was not of course sufficient to ensure Henry Warren's complete financial independence although his books sold well right through the restricted conditions of war-time publishing. Alongside were a number of more formal textbooks such as *Corn Country*, *Great Men of Essex*, *West Country*, *Footpath Through the Farm*, *Essex: The County Book* and an anthology of countryside prose and poetry called *The Good Life*. Henry's choices for this volume give us some idea of the literature which had influenced his view of rural matters – poets like John Clare, Andrew Young and William Cowper plus prose writers like Gilbert White, Izaak Walton, Richard Jefferies, W.H. Hudson, William Cobbett, Adrian Bell and H.J. Massingham. The fruitful output of this period of his life kept Henry going through into the 1950s. Although he had visited Austria before the war he now decided to spend a whole year there. *Tyrolean Journal* was the result.

At this period of his life Henry appreciated having friends nearby and these included Adrian Bell in Suffolk (where he had taken up farming) and Dodie Smith and her husband who were near neighbours and companions in the exploration of the Essex countryside where much of Henry's best writing took shape. He had the further advantage of attracting the best illustrators of his day to adorn his books. These included Denys Watkins-Pitchford, C.F. Tunnicliffe and Thomas Hennell.

INTRODUCTION

This time of peace and fruition was rudely shattered by economic difficulties. Writing is never a vocation that pays well and the fat years of success began to be swallowed up by lean years of failure. John Gili did his best by having some of Henry's later poems published in a collection called *The Thorn Tree* and this led to a broadcast on BBC Radio called *Countryman into Poet*, in which Henry reflected on his writing as it had come full circle from poetry through prose back to poetry again. But this barely affected the crisis he faced. Publishers in the 1960s were no longer interested in the sort of writing which C. Henry Warren had made his trademark. This was the era of 'white hot technology' and the television had now overtaken the radio as the primary medium of communication. The popular taste for his reflective essays and mellow broadcast talks had gone (happily only temporarily) out of fashion. On top of this came another blow when he was diagnosed as suffering from lung cancer, from which he died on 3 April 1966.

A renewed interest in his writing followed quite quickly after his death. First came *Content with What I Have* in which his best writing was collected together and illustrated by Susannah Holden. It was introduced by Richard Church who wrote a fitting tribute to Henry but who was to outlive him by only a few years. Henry Warren was regarded by Church as a twentieth-century Richard Jefferies and it had been this writer who had perhaps influenced Henry more than anyone. (Henry had edited and introduced a uniform edition of Jefferies' work in 1948.) In the 1970s there was little change in the attitude towards Henry's work, but in the 1980s a massive popular interest in the countryside began to develop, spearheaded by *The Country Diary of an Edwardian Lady* and a number of other similar books. As the decade went on a new sense of responsibility towards the environment spawned the current pre-occupation with Green issues. Thus three reprints came about as the book market responded to public concern about the endangering of the countryside and all things natural.

The most gratifying aspect of this has been the fulfilment of a cherished wish of Henry's which he never lived to see. In a letter to Richard Church just before his death he spoke of his intense desire to see *A Boy in Kent* and *A Cotswold Year* back in print. Thanks to Alan Sutton that has happened, and I was proud to write an introduction to the former. However this anthology is an attempt to put right a far more serious injustice. Its object is to display the variety and the quality of Henry Warren's prolific output. As I have reread the vast body of printed material to select the 'best' I have felt once again a degree of contact with my great-uncle, hearing his voice speaking through the printed page. I hope this choice of extracts truly does him justice and that he would have approved. But the acid test will be the response of old and new readers of Henry Warren for whom this volume has been prepared. The illustrations have been commissioned to bring the rather wide-ranging series of extracts together into one coherent book. The drawings are by John Cackett with whom I went to school.

Henry was truly the 'Contented Countryman' and over twenty-five years on from his death there has never been a greater need for the message which his books contain. We need in the midst of the technological revolution to pause long enough to hear writers like Henry Warren remind us about the true values of loyalty to the land and respect for nature which they received from their parents and grandparents and which we must pass on to our children and grandchildren. Henry Warren enjoyed a deep contentedness in the life he had chosen. He was fond of Bunyan's 'Song of the Shepherd Boy' from *A Pilgrim's Progress* (a book which his grandparents often read aloud to each other in their Hertfordshire cottage). Nothing better sums up how he would have wished to be remembered and it was these words he prefixed to his autobiography:

> He that is down needs fear no fall
> He that is low no pride
> He that is humble ever shall
> Have God to be his guide.
> I am content with what I have
> Little be it, or much –
> And Lord, contentment still I crave
> Because thou savest such.

Geoffrey R. Warren
1991

First the Blade
(1895–1918)

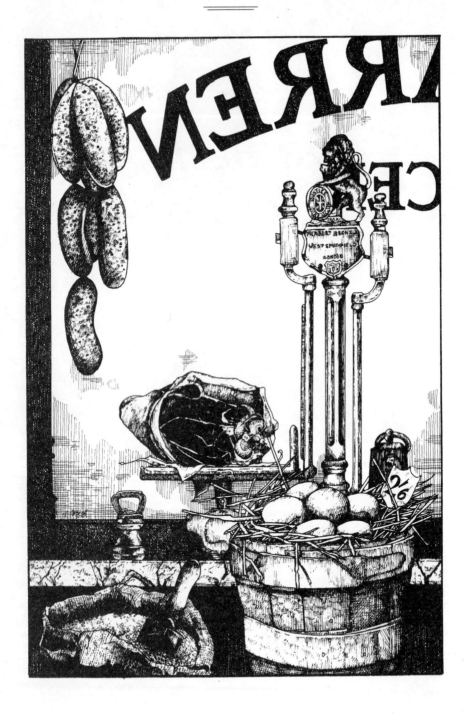

Hertfordshire Holidays

The best way in which I can hope to convey something of the cottage economy will be to tell of a particular cottage I knew fairly intimately as a boy – that time of life when, though we are unaware of it, we are receptive to detail as we never shall be again. Once every year I was taken to stay for a while with my paternal grandparents. Their diminutive cottage was already well on the way to being swallowed in the suburbs of the nearby town, and now it has disappeared altogether. But when I pass that way to-day in the train, as I sometimes do, it is not so much the sprawling town that I see from the carriage windows, with its congestion of houses and hardly a tree between, as my grandparents' tiny cottage, with its country smells and country ways – as if this would endure, in memory, when all these boxes of brick and mortar shall have fallen apart.

From the outside the cottage was nothing to look at: brick walls abutting on to the busy road, small windows out of which to peer at the passing traffic, and a slate roof. But even from the outside some hint was given of the neatness within by the flowered lace curtains and clean glass and whitened doorstep. All the garden was at the back of the cottage. It consisted of a long strip of ground, down the whole length of which, close against the dividing hedge of trim quick, ran a cobbled path. Never a weed was allowed to grow between those smooth, shiny cobbles that glistened in the rain and composed as good a garden path as any I have known. When he was over seventy, my grandfather would still get down on his knees (protected with a folded sack which he dragged with him inch by inch up the path) and dig out each tiny blade of grass with an old horn-handled dinner knife. Bordering the cobbled path there was a long row of clove carnations, my grandfather's pride and joy; and even to-day nothing will bring back the memory of that little garden, with its simple husbandry, like the fragrance of these favourite flowers.

Inside, everything was speckless – which is not at all to say that my grandmother was house-proud at the expense of full living: she was, indeed, within her necessarily narrow circumstances, as avid for experience as a bee for honey: it was simply that untidiness and its accompanying dirt would have meant confusion, and my grandparents could not afford confusion. I used to sleep in a little bedroom at the back of the cottage, and if I hung my head over the side of the bed I could just manage to see out of the window that was set almost at floor level. I would be wakened in the morning by the sounds of activity below – the pumping and splashing of water, the clatter of pans, the sizzling of bacon, the chatter of morning voices. Nothing was said or done in that cottage which could not be heard everywhere: one could also hear most of what went on next door. Intimacy, in fact, is the very characteristic of such cottages; and while, in some instances, it may lead to coarseness and sluttery, in others it leads to orderliness and a general simplicity of behaviour: it all depends upon the essential nature of the cottagers concerned. Everything in its place and a place for everything: this is a sheer necessity in cottage life. Thus, through the generations, these limitations of space, coupled with small earnings, have induced in the best kind of cottager a ritual of conduct based on neatness and simplicity: a discipline having its foundation in compulsion but none the less admirable in effect for that. To the cottager of the good old school, waste was a major sin.

But the room I remember best in my grandparents' cottage was the little front room. It was the work-room, living-room, dining-room, parlour, and everything else. I marvel now when I think of the multitude of activities it adapted itself to in the course of the week without once losing that modest dignity and comfort which were the unspoken pleasure of all who entered it. These might range from squire to roadman, parson to grocer's boy: whoever they were, they could not help but feel at home the moment they entered. It seems to me as if, whenever I was there, a continual flow of visitors of one sort or another came into that little room. Perhaps my grandmother, seated in her wheelback armchair in the chimney corner, would be shelling a bowl of peas in her lap. Whatever she was doing, she never laid aside her task for long out of deference to a caller. The routine of the morning must go its accustomed way, or she would never get through all the things that had to be done before the day was out. Nor did she ever apologize: indeed, there was no need. Peeling potatoes or polishing the grate, ironing shirts or pouring out tea, she ever maintained that natural dignity which is beyond the prerogative of class. Quality, I realize to-day, was the hall-mark of the tiny cottage and all that went on there. It proclaimed itself even in the cottage furniture – the polished tripod table, smooth as glass, the corner cupboard, with its lustre jug and Lowestoft china, the old carved chest, smelling of lavender bags when it was opened, the severe wooden chairs, well-turned and comely, and the grandfather clock wheezing in the corner. But most it proclaimed itself in the owners and users of these things.

Somehow it was my grandmother who, all day, dominated the scene. Perhaps the reason for this was simply that, in the daytime, my grandfather would be out and about a great deal. But when evening came he took the centre of the simple stage. With her hands folded quiet at last on her black silk apron and her evening lace cap on her head, my grandmother would sit attentively listening while he read aloud to her. Invariably those readings followed the same course: a bit or two out of the newspaper, a letter that must be read over again and discussed, and then, to finish up with, a few pages from a favourite book. I do not suppose there were more than half-a-dozen books all told in that cottage, for the only schooling the old couple had ever known was a dame school for which their parents paid a penny or two a week. And of that half-dozen I am only certain now of one. It always seems to have been the same book from which my grandfather read, at least when I was there. I did not know much about the meaning of faith in those days, but now I should not hesitate to say that my grandparents were its humble and whole-hearted exponents. And I think it must have been the fervour and actuality which my grandfather managed to put into his reading of the trials and endurances of Christian that has identified Bunyan's immortal book with him in my mind, so that all the well-known passages seem to say themselves to me in his voice, the while I see my grandmother sitting by, listening, her eyes curtained behind their delicately veined lids.

Father and Son

When the last lights had been blown out in the shop, and everybody had gone home, my father used to pull down the door-blinds and set in its sockets a cumbersome iron bar calculated, if need be, to keep out the stoutest intruder. I felt very secure, hearing the iron clanking into place. That burglars might prefer an easier way in, such as a window, never occurred to me. Silence and darkness closed over the shop – a darkness filled with the scents of soap and bacon, calico and cheese. Only the light in the little office burned on. Thither, if his accounts were not yet finished, my father would retire, perch himself on his high stool, and be lost for a while in the difficult mazes of his figures.

Whenever I thought the circumstances at all propitious, I would hang about, hoping that the invitation for which I was waiting would come at last, when, quiet as a mouse, I could sidle into the forbidden room. Once inside, I knew that I was safe so long as I kept quiet: the trouble was to get inside. It was an irresistible attraction to me to be shut in that tiny cube of light with my father, the scented darkness outside, and no sound but the scratching of his pen and the muttering of many numbers. For a time I was content to lean against the files and ledgers in there, watching, dreaming. Maybe my father only pretended not to know I was there: anyway, he took no notice of me. Then, as noiselessly as I could, I pulled the drawers out of their nest, one by one, fingering and toying with the grubby treasures that were inside. I knew the contents of each little drawer by heart, but familiarity could never make them less delightful to me. I do not know why my childish fancy should have chosen to invest these paltry oddments with such a glow and glamour. Perhaps it was because I so rarely had the opportunity to finger them. Perhaps it was because I knew that they had belonged to my father's own childhood. Once he had told me all about them, holding them up in the yellow lamplight, relishing again the pleasures of an earlier day; and now they were my passport back into those Hertfordshire lanes and meadows where he had played as a boy.

In one drawer there was a cigar-box filled with faded birds' eggs lying cushioned in sawdust. The varnish had diminished their delicate colours to a dirty, uniform brown, and the names that had been carefully written upon them had all but worn away. But there were no specimens in my own small collection that could compare with these in my eyes. These were eggs of fabulous birds from a country I had never known and a day far back before I was born. When I had had my fill of them, I settled them securely in their bed of sawdust again and shut the drawer. Another compartment, I remember, contained an uncatalogued assortment of old coins, tarnished and worn, the royal heads greened with mildew.

But my keenest interest was in yet another drawer, which I always saved to the last. These others, with their coins and eggs and so forth, were only the prelude, setting the mood, conducting my imagination into that vague but fascinating world of my father's youth. This last drawer contained nothing less than the fragment of a thunderbolt. So, at any rate, I had been told when the rough bit of stone was first put into my hand. It had fallen during a storm the like of which, I was assured, I had never seen and, pray God, never should see. People had been killed and great trees shivered into a thousand pieces. Out of the blackened sky this iron stone had fallen, burying itself deep in a garden near by. It was a visitation from heaven – no less. Holding the grim half-ball in the cup of my hand, I looked at its smooth, shining core: harder than granite it seemed, brighter than polished marble. It was solidified fire, my father said, a bolt hurled by God as a warning into this sinful world. 'But of His infinite mercy,' he went on, his voice subdued in awe and gratitude, 'He saw to it that none of our dear ones was hurt.' I was profoundly stirred. Could it really be that this thing I held in my hand had once been closed within the hand of God and thrown in anger out of the skies? I put it back in the drawer and stood there lost awhile in a dream of wonder. Nothing I had ever heard the village clergyman say, shaking his finger at us in admonition, as he leaned out of the pulpit, had ever brought home to me, like this iron-grey fragment of a thunderbolt, the miraculous blend of wrath and mercy that was Jehovah. But at last the dream was shattered by my father's voice as he laid down his pen and shook out his pipe in the palm of his hand. 'Come along,' he said; 'I think we've done quite enough for one day, don't you?' And when he had blown vigorously down the chimney of the lamp, to put out the flame, we walked together through the aromatic darkness of the shop in to supper. And while I lay abed that night, waiting for sleep, I wondered if I should ever see God's fury working among men, as my father had done, and whether, like him, I should be spared.

Greetings to
Mereworth School

I am grateful to the Headmaster for this opportunity to salute the school which, so to speak, started me on my way. That was a long time ago; and I am sure the school is a very different place today from what it was when I attended it, before going on to Maidstone Grammar School. Indeed, you may have some idea of how long ago it was if I tell you one or two of the odd things that sprang to mind when I received the Headmaster's letter suggesting that I should write a foreword to your magazine on the occasion of the school's centenary.

I remembered, for instance, the morning hymn with which the whole school started every day. It sounded more like a lament for lost freedom than praise for a new day about to begin. All the classroom doors were left open: even so, some of the classes invariably lagged behind a bar or two, and the effect was far from musical. . . . I remembered too, the hum, like a roomful of bees, when we were set to learn some verses by heart (it must have been mostly pretence, for I have long since forgotten the verses). . . . I found myself recalling the peeling bricks in the wall where I would sometimes be stood in a corner, with my hands folded on my head, like a ton weight, for what seemed hours on end – a punishment that surely exceeded any crime of which I was capable. . . . I even seemed to hear again the quick swish of the cane as it descended on my upturned palm – what had I been up to that time, I wonder? . . . And how closely must I have watched the big clock on the wall as the hands slowly stole the hours away, for I found myself recalling its face, and stuttering tick. . . . But perhaps my most vivid recollection was of how, after another hymn to close the day, we raced through the porch like a pack of hyenas released from their cage, grabbing our caps and coats (or somebody else's) and tumbling pell-mell out of the gate into the open roadway – free at last.

However, you would be quite wrong if you were to suppose from all this that my school-days at Mereworth must have been very unpleasant. Far from it. It is everybody's privilege to overlook the good he got from his school-days and concentrate upon the bad; so you need not pity me too much. In fact, I will put it this way: in spite of everything I enjoyed myself quite a lot – but at the same time I am sure that I should have enjoyed myself a great deal more if I could somehow have changed places with you today, who have all sorts of schooltime amenities and advantages that were never even dreamed of when I was a boy.

So my advice to you (if I may dare to offer such a thing), is that you 'go to it' with all your might and get the best out of every day. There is an old Chinese saying that puts the matter very well: 'Enjoy yourself. It is later than you think.'

Five Acre Field

I knew it simply as 'The Meadow'. If to others, perhaps, the name might have sounded too assuming for so modest a pasture, to me at least it had no such pretentiousness. I knew other meadows in plenty, and no doubt they were often much bigger and better, but for me there was only one meadow that mattered. Its appeal was intimate and secret. I felt quite possessive about it; and though of course others often shared it with me, for play or picnic, nutting or blackberrying, I was well aware that these were not the occasions that really counted. The Meadow yielded up its full measure of joy to me only when I went into it alone. At no other time did it fully come alive.

The key was kept on a piece of string threaded through a large 'lucky' pebble, worn as smooth as marble; and with this clutched tightly in the palm of my hand, I would run down the Street feeling that I was about to enter into the possession of my kingdom. When I had reached the gate I would turn the key in the rusty lock, fasten it again on the inside, and carefully conceal the pebble and key under the trailing briars by the gate-post. It never occurred to me that nobody else could possibly want to come in: I only knew that I should not feel quite so secure in the enjoyment of my secret if I left the lock unfastened. By the action of turning the key I had drawn an invisible cloak over me. It did not matter now that on one side the Meadow was open to the full gaze of at least half a dozen houses in the Street or that anybody who happened to be passing by could see quite clearly what was going on. I had shut the world away.

In shape the Meadow was roughly like a top-boot, with the heel and toe farthest away from the Street. In size it was about five acres, as I learned one day when I saw it picked out on a large-scale survey map, with the words 'Five Acre Meadow' written across it in a thin violet script. Ever after I was to measure acres in terms of the Meadow. 'Mr Leaf has got fifty acres laid down with winter wheat this year,' somebody would say; and at once I was trying to imagine ten top-boots, each the size of the Meadow, all lumped together in one big field. It was the only measurement I had to go by, for the Five Acre Meadow was all we ever possessed in the way of land. And every square yard of it was treasure to me.

Though all sorts of important things have since been forgotten, I can still remember the smallest details of the Meadow. Just there was where the ash-tree grew, and almost opposite it, on the other side, grew the oak: by which I used to test, year after year, a country rhyme I had once been told, 'Oak before ash, We shall have a splash; Ash before oak, We shall have a soak!' Not far from the oak grew a wild cherry-tree, a joy in spring, when it scattered its petals on the grass, and a joy again in autumn, when it thrust out boughs spattered with blood. Then there were the horse-chestnut trees, from which each year I gathered my own store of 'conkers', boring holes through them with a red-hot skewer so that they should not split, and hoping, vainly, that one of them might yet prove to be the champion of the village. Even the hedges were known to me intimately, yard by yard. This was where the hazels yielded the sweetest nuts and that was where the sloes grew largest. Here I was sure to find a blackbird's nest among the thicker boughs, and there, where the ditch was packed with a litter of dead leaves, it would be unusual if I did not find a robin's nest or a wren's. One knot of bushes was made memorable for me by the discovery of a long-tailed-tit's nest; and I remember now my concern as to how a bird with so long a tail could ever contrive to get itself turned round in a nest whose mossy mouth was only just big enough to admit two of my fingers pressed close together – let alone the question of bringing up a family of ten or eleven in it.

Perhaps it was birds'-nesting that taught me most about the Meadow. With an easy intentness that eludes us as we grow older, I could discover nests in the most secretive places. I used to carry the eggs home in the peak of my cap, and great was the disgust of Mary, our maid-of-all-work, when I proceeded to 'blow' them over the kitchen sink. Sometimes they would be slightly set, and then a curious mixture of blood and yoke bubbled out of the pin-hole. 'Take 'em away!' Mary would shout at me. 'Take 'em away! You dirty little scaramouch!' And I was compelled to retreat to the yard to continue my delicate operations there.

One section of the hedge in the Meadow was rank with elderberries and nettles, exhaling a smell that was always subtly repellent to me. Wild musk grew in the ditch at another point, where, even in summer, there was a thin trickle of water; and I would fit the spotted yellow hoods over my finger, smoothing them down tightly, till they split and fell off. Close at hand fig-wort abounded, a flower that seemed to me foolishly insignificant for so tall and succulent a stem; and mares' tails, that began life as a bare, stunted stalk and ended it as a great plume of long green needles. I knew where the first sprays of honeysuckle were to be found and where the first wild roses: in autumn I would select the reddest hips and set them gracefully in trailing old man's beard, making the bouquet rare with one or two furry robins' pincushions and carrying it home in triumph. I knew the nature of the various grasses and even the Meadow's dips and mounds. I knew it exactly, in every season and at every hour. And I knew these things not by virtue of that meticulous observation which adults use, but by active contact, careless of aesthetic pleasure, knowing only that here was a world awaiting my discovery, a world for hands and eyes and ears to explore at every turn.

No wonder, then, if I was possessive in my enjoyment. 'Findings, keepings,' we used to say, after the a-moral manner of children; and who but I had 'found' the Meadow?

But it was the toe of the Meadow that always gave me the greatest joy. Mushrooms might grow elsewhere, so that I could come down with my basket early in the morning, searching among the 'fairy rings' that showed up so darkly in the gleaming grass, snipping off the cool, satiny buttons that were half buried in the earth until my nails were clotted with dirt, and taking special care not to break the larger ones that had already ripened to blackness on the flaky under sides. Or blackberries might prosper on the hedges nearer the Street, so that, with the aid of a long, crooked stick that I kept specially for the purpose, I could gather all the fruit I could possibly need, until my lips were black and my fingers juicy red, without even bothering to range farther afield. But still it was the toe of the Meadow, devoid of mushrooms and unable to boast anything better in the way of hedge-fruit than a few flavourless dewberries, that I liked best; for it was there that I used to clamber through a thorny gap in the hedge and enter the copse. Once there, I was well out of sight and sound of the church clock or any other pertinent reminder of that busy world where things went by the rule of Shall and Must. Though I might often share the Meadow with friends, I do not remember ever sharing the copse; yet nowhere was I less alone.

Boy into Poet

It's an old prank with schoolboys and I remember when I was a boy how we used to get one up on the English master by substituting lines of our own in the poetry recitation. One particular favourite was Tennyson's 'Ballad of Oriano'. Everywhere the line has the refrain 'Oriano', this is how it sounded the way we said it –

> 'The cock was crowing on the wall
> Upside down . . .' etc.

It was something more than a joke. It was a way of showing our contempt for the whole business of poetry . . . a feeble sort of occupation for a boy. Of course I joined in the joke but privately I held a quite different point of view. It was poetry, even at school, that most readily gripped my attention and I can't remember the time when I wasn't writing my own poetry. Naturally I kept it a secret as if it were a vice of some sort and then one day there arrived at the school a temporary English master to do duty while our regular one was away ill. Somehow or other he discovered my addiction and he had the wit and intelligence enough to actually encourage me in the interest.

Like a plant that's been kept in the dark and then is suddenly brought out into the sunlight, poetry instantly began to thrive in me to become the robust and natural thing it ought to be. And if now I can say that it is one of the most rewarding things in life, I owe that gift largely to the temporary English master whose name even I have forgotten. As for the poetry I wrote in those early days I'm sure it was pretty poor stuff. All the same the writing of it taught me a delight in the handling of words and sharpened my senses. It opened my eyes and ears to the world I was growing up in. That world was a country one, in the deep Kentish countryside and there was one little corner of it which became for me especially associated with poetry. Beyond the village there was a hill crested by a clump of towering beech trees. It was called the Hurst and from it could be seen miles around. It was intensely important and exciting for me. Even today though I have never returned, I can track every yard of the winding lane that leads up to it. My senses were so stretched full of anticipation, I would sit down between the roots of one of the largest of the beech trees, lean my back against the trunk and gaze out over miles and miles of the Kentish Weald. I felt on top of the world not only because of the view. I felt like this because I was enjoying the thing I best liked doing – the making of poetry. In an old exercise book I used to write down odds and ends of verses as I invented them – if that's the right word – on my walks alone or cycling to school or when I was supposed to be learning my homework, the binomial theorem or the contents of the Bill of Rights.

And now up there on the windy Hurst I would work on them, trying to finish them, shaping the fragments into a satisfying whole; satisfying is the operative word, saying the lines over and over, adding and taking away, altering them until they were exactly as I liked them to sound saying exactly what I wanted them to say. It was a more satisfying occupation than any I knew. I didn't realize at the time of course that this satisfaction was really the joy that comes from creating. I was creating something which until then had never existed. I was giving words life. In fact a boy was growing into a poet.

A Quick Change
Library

My father owned the General Stores in Mereworth, selling everything from groceries to bread, drapery to paraffin, wines and spirits, newpapers and magazines. The shop was also the village Post Office. Only in one part of the whole concern had I any interest whatever and that was the Newsagency – not the daily papers, which anyhow I had nothing to do with – but the weeklies and magazines which arrived in the shop on Friday evening and were at once a source of the greatest interest to me. I awaited the arrival of the village carrier's van as if it was bringing in the rarest merchandise. Frequent stops along the seven miles journey out of Maidstone meant that it never reached the shop until late in the evening and sometimes indeed, the shop had been shut (eight o'clock was shutting-up time) and we were having supper when we heard the carrier's old horse pull up before the door and the carrier himself (probably tipsy) stumble out of the van, fasten the nosebag on the horse, and come rattling the shop door latch. I would accompany my father through the shop, turn up the lamps while he slid the great iron safety bars out, and then hang about while the carrier brought in the day's goods, waiting for one particular moment. Of all the goods he brought – sides of bacon, crates of beer, sacks of sugar, parcels of this and bags of that – the only ones I waited for and gave a hand with, were the great rolls of weekly papers and magazines which arrived every Friday. As soon as the carrier had tossed them on to the store-room counter, I took a bacon knife and cut the strings that held the rolls together. Most of the contents were wads of local newspapers, still smelling of printer's ink, but in these I was not interested; and although I was expected to give a hand in folding them ready for the roundsman to take out on Saturday, I did so in a sort of mechanical stupor, anxious for the time to come when the last newspaper would be laid on the mounting heaps and I was at last free to take my first glance at the weeklies. These assorted magazines and periodicals fascinated me and provided me with a quick-change library of extraordinary catholicity.

I had my favourites among them, of course, including *Country Life*, *Illustrated London News*, *Bazaar*, *Exchange and Mart*, *Strand Magazine*, *The Captain*, *Police News*, *Home Chat* and others I have now forgotten even the names of. At that age youth's appetite for knowledge is enormous, and perhaps what is wanted is not so much quality as quantity. Instinct (if not intelligence) will enable the youth to sort out the grain — his particular choice of grain — from the chaff. In this unusual access to so large a quantity of printed matter, therefore, I was extremely lucky. When others, remembering their own youth, tell me of the books which they were brought up on, often having them read aloud and anyway always available on the family's well-stocked shelves, I do not regret the lack of such a cultural atmosphere in my own home. Indeed, I feel only gratitude that things were as they were, since, with access to that plethora of papers and magazines, I had to do my own sorting out, hunt for my own favourites, forge my own critical (or anyway selective) values.

It seemed to me, on those Friday nights, that I had scarcely got my nose into those magazines when I was snatched away and told to get upstairs to bed. Still I was happy with just the promise of the riches they contained — to turn the thick shiny pages of *Country Life* or *Illustrated London News* savouring a picture here, a tit-bit of news there, was of itself an enchantment. The real enjoyment, however, would come tomorrow, when I would shut myself in the store-room, pick and choose as I wanted to and gloat at leisure. In some of the magazines were serials whose next instalment I had waited for all week, only to have the paper whipped out of my hand because a customer had called for his copy and was waiting for it in the shop. Serials, however could be caught up with next week by reading the synopsis; but many a short story was lost to me in this way, taken out of my hands just as I was reaching the climax. Maybe it was frustrating; maybe it was even harmful. I don't know but I do know the dim store-room with its peculiar odour of cheese and bacon, sawdust and newsprint, was a weekend sanctum for me, where in private I fed my mind with snippets of this and snatches of that – a hotch-potch of ready matter that was not the less exciting (and in its way even important) for being so scrappy and haphazard. The store-room was my library and I can never estimate its significance in my youthful development for the varied vistas it opened for me into a world as yet untried.

Through the Eyes of a Child

The window of my bedroom looked out on to the bakehouse, and every morning, long before anybody else was awake, I could hear George, the baker, whistling to himself as he thumped the dough in the troughs or raked the wood-ash out of the oven. I do not remember what were the tunes he whistled, but I do remember how shrill and vibrant they sounded in the stillness of early morning. It seemed as if they must be heard all over the village.

George was a lusty sort of fellow, and so perhaps he could not bear the peace and fragility of those hours round about dawn: something had to be done to make them seem less lonely. He thumped the dough as if it were a punch-ball; he sent the bread-tins clattering over the floor; and he clanked the iron rakers against the brick walls of the oven with a ferocity quite out of proportion to the needs of the task. And, as I have said, he whistled.

Often there were mornings when I slept through all the din going on in the bakehouse, but there were many other mornings when I lay awake listening, giving to every noise its appropriate cause, watching with my mind's eye every movement of that solitary man. Sometimes I felt that I could lie there no longer: imagination was not enough. Then I would slide out of bed, tip-toe across the cold linoleum, and peer through the strip of lace curtain that was stretched across the lower half of the window.

I did not feel that I was eavesdropping. I felt that I was being present at some secret drama, in which George was the sole actor and I the sole audience; and I wanted to keep it a secret. So I knelt there, shivering on the wooden chair beside the window, and stared through the peacocks and the flower-baskets on the curtain at the familiar activities over the way. If George had seen me, he would have called up to me and started a conversation, for from the first day of his arrival as 'the new baker' a friendly bond had existed between us. But that was not what I wanted: it would have spoiled the whole show. I preferred to watch in secret.

Perhaps it was winter, and the yard below was still dark. I would hear him greasing the tins and throwing them from one side of the bakehouse to the other while he whistled his strident tunes. Then suddenly the door would open. Light poured over the yard. Away at the back of the bakehouse I could see a fierce red glow in the open mouth of the oven. George was raking out the ashes; and as he did so, they fell in sparkling showers around his feet. When he had finished, he took a damping-cloth, wound it loosely over the end of a pole, dropped it in a bucket of water, and then swirled it wildly round the inside of the oven, so that it spluttered and hissed and steamed and made a fine to-do. Cleaning the oven, however, was only the occupation of a few minutes. Too soon the bakehouse door was shut again and the yard was hidden in darkness. But still I would wait beside the window, the cold surface of the chair numbing my knees, as if after all this was only an interval in the course of the play and must be endured with patience.

Or perhaps it was summer, and I was at the window even earlier in the morning. The white clematis that covered the whole of one end of the bakehouse foamed in blossom over the wall. The roof, spattered with rich bosses of lichen and moss, cut a sharp line against the faint blue of the clean, new sky. I could hear birds singing in the garden and everything seemed extraordinarily bright. Dozens of large faggots were propped against the high wall that joined up to the bakehouse and formed the boundary of the yard. George came out and selected one, hoisting it on to his broad shoulders as if it were as light as a sack of feathers. I watched him with boyish admiration. His trousers were white and ragged round his boots, his big wrists and knuckles were caked with dough, and his hair, that was still ruffled from the pillow, was powdered with flour. But he did not seem to me in the least grotesque. I much preferred this early-morning guise to the immaculate figure I knew he would cut later in the day, when he appeared fresh from his second sleep, his trousers brushed, his cap tilted at a saucy angle, his hair greased and shiny, and only the doughy rims of his finger-nails still revealing the trade he had followed at dawn. He took the faggot and rammed it into the oven. He came out into the yard to fetch another. And then another. And every time, somewhere at the back of my mind was the thought that hidden in one of those faggots there might be a birds' nest, filled, maybe, with little naked birds. For once, when the faggots were running low, and some came to light that had never been uncovered for a year, I had found a nest with five pale-blue eggs in it; and thereafter every faggot was looked on by me as a potential home for robins and wrens.

So the drama went on, always the same, always entrancing. Kneeling at the window, time did not exist for me. But presently I would hear the maid come out from the kitchen to pump water, the handle squeaking at every jerk; or Alfred, the yard-man, would clump over the cobbles with his hob-nailed boots, lift the latch of the stable-door, and give his regular greeting to the mares; 'Marnin', Dolly! Marnin', Betty!' And I would go back to my warm bed. The play was over for that day.

East End Invaders

Once every year, in September, Mereworth suffered an invasion. For days the village would be busy preparing for the defence. The four chief publicans, for instance, laid in large quantities of beer. Slow drays lumbered up to the inns; the cellar doors were flung open; and fat, leather-aproned drivers rolled barrel after barrel down into the echoing interiors. Then again, the farmers put every available man on to stripping the plum-trees and picking all the apples that were ripe enough. They also filled up every gap in their hedges and put new stakes in the broken-down fences.

But the preparations that most interested me were those made by my father. Down in the chilly cellar under the shop, Dutch cheeses, like bright-red cannon-balls, were piled in tremendous pyramids. The miller, wearing a white sack over his head, like a Carmelite friar, came stumbling up the yard with so much flour that George's meal-shed was soon crammed to the door. Sacks of sugar were stacked in another shed, and as I passed by I could hear the sated wasps buzzing there in hundreds. And all day Alfred seemed to be winding and unwinding the squealing, primitive handcrane that carried crates and boxes and bags from the yard up into the warehouse.

In the shop itself the stir and bustle were just as frantic. First of all everything was cleared away, until not so much as a jar of sweets or a tin of treacle was left within reach, and even in the windows there was nothing but a swept-up heap of dead wasps in a corner. Then, after the shop had been scrubbed from top to bottom, Horace, the odd-job man, would arrive with planks and poles and hammer and nails and begin erecting a high barricade round the counters. The place rattled with his vigorous hammerings: the lamps shook and the dead wasps danced in the window. And when the barricade was ready, my father came along and hit it here and kicked it there to make quite sure it was strong enough to defend him and his assistants against the coming onslaught.

'I think we could do with just a few more nails here, Horace,' he would say; 'or we shall have the hooligans all over us in a trice!'

At last the preparations were considered adequate, and everybody settled down to await the invaders' arrival, filling in the time by weighing up endless packets of tea and sugar in blue dunces' caps and stacking them neatly on the shelves and under the counters.

These, however, were only the last-minute preparations: less ostensibly, other parts of Mereworth had been getting ready for months. The village lay in the centre of the Kentish hop-growing district, and for nearly three-quarters of the year a large percentage of the land was bare save for a complicated system of poles and wires and string that netted the hop-gardens from hedge to hedge. No orchard trees were tended with half the care that Mereworth devoted to its hop-bines. As soon as they appeared out of the ground, the tender shoots were nursed and pinched and thinned. Men on long stilts picked their way down the narrow alleys between the poles, tightening the cross-pieces of wire and threading the miles of manila string that was needed to carry each slender bine from earth to sky. The ground around the plants was kept free from weeds, and every now and then yellow clouds of sulphur would float across the roads as the bines were sprayed against the blight of rust or aphis.

Of all these complicated preparations the invaders themselves neither knew nor cared. Mostly they came from the East End of London, and Mereworth meant little more to them than an outlandish place somewhere in the country, where the inhabitants were terribly slow, where bulls might be met with unexpectedly in the fields, and where in September you could earn good money picking hops. What the village looked like during the rest of the year they had no idea, all country matters being essentially outside their direct experience. They knew only that for four or five weeks they would work by day in the hop-gardens and sleep by night in the huts and tents provided for them by the farmers. In between times there would be a great deal of noisy fun.

But for us the arrival of these invaders was the prelude to complete disruption. Mereworth was turned upside down. The first of them came on foot, a dreary vanguard pushing perambulators heaped to twice their height with bulky bundles, a kettle and a saucepan clattering away somewhere underneath, and a tin bath piled on the top. They were the 'casuals', men and women who had not been expressly hired by the farmers beforehand but who came drifting into the village in the hope of finding work, and who, if they did not find it, moved on disconsolately to the next.

About the same time, too, came those whom we called the 'toffs'. We said they came early so that they might secure the pick of the huts; but they said it was so that they might enjoy a few days' holiday in the country before the riff-raff arrived to spoil everything. Such, notably, were the Jones family. They travelled down by the ordinary passenger train, complete with beds and bedding, trunks and crockery, and even wallpaper. They would immediately present themselves at the shop, dressed in feathers and silks, and ask after our family's health with the most intimate concern. I listened while Mrs Jones crammed a year's news into a few minutes, but my interest was more in her strong cockney accent than in the things she said.

'We couldn't keep away after all, you see,' she would say, fumbling in the depths of a large, shining handbag and clinking a jumble of coins there. 'It does us all such a lot of good. We did think we'd go to Margate instead this year, but in the end we all decided the hop-fields are better medicine than any amount of sea air. If only there weren't so many rowdies!'

The Piano in the Front Room

That we had a piano at home, when I was a boy, did not mean that we were a musical family. Far from it. The family consisted of my father and mother, my two older brothers and myself; and (heaven knows why – and I mean heaven) I was the only one who showed the slightest interest in music. Nor have I been able to discover any musical aptitude farther back in the family, either on my mother's or my father's side. As my father owned the General Stores, our status in the community was poised somewhat precariously between those who had pretentions to 'class' and those who were free from any such aspirations. Naturally we aimed to climb to the higher rather than sink to the lower, and so the piano in the first place may well have been purchased to emphasize the family ambitions. It would be a sign that we were at least on the way up, since at that time just prior to the First World War, a piano was as much a symbol of social position as a motor car was just before the Second World War. It also had its value, of course, as furniture. Not that it was one of those ornate instruments, all fretwork and faded green silk. It was, indeed, a plain and substantial upright grand, with a pleasant tone and (what I am sure was much more important in my mother's eyes) a polish like glass, the sort of 'piece' in fact that would have done any family credit.

Unfortunately the only place it could occupy in the room chosen to house it was against the wall furthest from the window, so that the pianist sat in his own light. Matters did not even improve after dark, when the curtains were drawn and the lamp lighted, for the latter was suspended on chains from the middle of the ceiling and so cast still darker shadow on one's music. Admittedly there were two brass sconces on the front of the piano which would have done something to relieve the gloom, but it was forbidden to light the candles in them (except on special occasions, such as Christmas, when they were allowed to add to the festive scene), for fear of spilling grease on the keys. Finally on top of the piano were several framed photographs, a marble clock with a vigorous tick and some painted glass vases whose jangling was not appreciably diminished by the home-made woolly mats fringed with bobbles and pink flowers on which they stood. All this should have been more of a nuisance to me, the piano's only user, than in fact it was. What I did find a nuisance (and its effects probably went quite deep) was the almost total lack of privacy I enjoyed whenever I played the piano. The piano was in a room called by courtesy the dining-room; and it is true that we ate our meals there; but it also served many other purposes, from play-room to work-room and convenient meeting room for all and sundry. It had three doors (no wonder the candles were not allowed to be lighted) and was about as public as a room could well be.

One door led to the kitchen, where, if the maid-of-all-work was not clattering her pails and dishes, the weekly washer-woman was pummeling clothes in the copper and filling the house with clouds of steam. The second door opened (when the plush curtain had been pulled aside, the bolts drawn and the great key turned in its lock) to the yard and side-entrance. Here the shop-vans were drawn up to be loaded with bread and groceries for the day-long rounds into neighbouring villages. This seemed to involve everybody on the premises – and several village lads besides. Moreover the din they made was increased by the fact that the yard entrance burrowed under the first floor of the house and was shut off from the road by two enormous wooden doors. Everything echoed there as in a tunnel. The horses whinnied impatiently in the shafts; George, the baker, whistled the latest music-hall ditties while Alfred, the yard-man, supplied the words in a lusty tenor; and odd-job Horace bawled at the boys to scare them off but only succeeded in making them bawl back at him. Altogether it would have needed more than bolts and locks and curtains to keep out such a din. In a way, however, it was the third door that offered the most serious obstacle to my privacy. It led into the shop and there was practically always somebody either going in or coming out. Moreover it usually stood ajar, which meant that anybody who happened to be in the shop at the time could hear me playing. I should have thought that this would have been a nuisance to those serving behind the counter, but perhaps they liked music while they worked. As for my father himself, poring over his account books in the office behind the shop, I don't suppose he was even aware of my playing for he never showed any signs that he heard it any other times and would sleep soundly in his armchair by the fire through the wildest of fortissimos.

The Church on the Hill

I have spoken before of that little church on a hill, lonely among the trees, approached up a long sunken lane on whose ivied banks the first primroses always were to be found. Those early primroses must have been important to me for they have remained vividly in my mind, so bland and fragrant among the moss and marbled ivy leaves, as if they were a symbol of the joy I knew I was nearing with every step of the climb to East Peckham Church. This joy had nothing whatever to do with religion or worship; it sprung entirely from my sense of expectation. The church was so remotely situated that Sunday evensong was always sung in the afternoon, since few indeed would have braved those lanes after dark. This fact provided my parents with a respectable excuse, especially in spring, for a pleasant Sunday afternoon walk. Like most country people in those days, they used the opportunity of a Sunday holiday for a leisurely viewing of crops and gardens; but the walk to East Peckham Church had an additional attraction in that it provided a welcome rest at the end of the climb and a comfortable downhill jog home afterwards to the substantial Sunday tea. I too enjoyed the walk – though less for its own sake than for the drama (it was hardly less) which I knew would be its climax once we had filed through the old timbered porch and taken our places in the pine pews. I walked along in an expectation of enchantment for in truth that is the effect Canon Ryley's voice, speaking or singing, had upon·me.

By any reckoning he was a remarkable man. It still seems strange to me that one so richly endowed should have chosen a tiny country church with only a handful of worshippers. He could have commanded attention, one would have thought, in a cathedral; indeed, in earlier days he had done so. But now, he lived shut away in a rook-haunted vicarage, miles from anywhere. Could it have been that he was by preference a quietist? Did his nature demand for its proper fulfilment a withdrawal from the world so that he might cultivate his talent in a way suited to its limitations? It rather looks like this to me now. All I do know is that, whatever the cause, I for one benefited enormously by the consequences.

His talent was for music. As a minor Canon in one of the West Country cathedrals he must have found plenty of scope for its employment in the various musical activities of the district, not least of which, of course, was the Three Choirs Festival, whose performances I was later to hear him speak of, again and again, with a nostalgia that communicated itself even to me, a boy for whom the event was only an item in the news. Then why had he forsaken so congenial an atmosphere and come to live in East Peckham, where however quick the people might be to appreciate him as a man and as their vicar, they certainly could not have had any sensible appreciation of him as a musician? Not that he didn't give them any occasion to do so. For all the handicap of no organist and nothing much in the way of an organ (and soon less in the way of a choir), the musical part of East Peckham's church services was arresting. It proclaimed the ability of genius to triumph over the lack of any suitable material to work on. It owed its appeal, first and foremost, to the Canon's own resonantly tuneful voice. In the absence of choir and organ, he not only led the hymns and psalms, but sang them practically solo. Bemused by that strong (to say the truth, rather lush) voice, soon those in the congregation who might have joined in, rarely did so more than *sotto voce*, as if they wished not to spoil the effect. And there was a second reason for the appeal of the musical part of the service. Because he was a fine musician, he allowed nothing tawdry; simple the music had to necessarily be, but it was also good.

Sufficient Amends

I had my lessons and did my practising on the little organ at our parish church. Mostly my practising had to be done in the evening, after my school home-work was finished and put away. To find a blower to accompany me was not difficult, since most of the village boys I knew were glad to pick up a penny or two, and anyway the job itself — especially on dark winter evenings — was not without a certain dramatic appeal. Not one of them would have entered the church alone at night, for fear of they knew not what; and certainly I would not have done so myself without some trepidation. With each other for company, however, there was even a horrid attraction about the experience. My most frequent blower was Fred, not because he was more adept than the other aspirants to the honour, but simply because he lived nearby and was therefore handy to come by at a moment's notice. When I had scrambled through my school preparation I would grab my music and a lantern, and, with this swinging at my knees and making a catherine-wheel of light around my feet, I would hurry off to Fred's cottage. If I had warned him in advance the door would open as soon as I lifted the latch of the garden gate and a sudden rectangle of fire and flame-given light revealed half-a-dozen faces peering into the dark — it was Fred and his raggle-taggle little brothers and sisters. 'You want me to blow?' he would yell, and without waiting for my answer would come clattering with his hob-nailed boots down the cobbled path. Together we plunged into the dark night, made darker presently by the thick avenue of yew trees that lined the approach to the church. An enormous key was kept behind the notice board and leaning the weight of both hands on this, Fred wound it into the lock and there we were, in the long echoing nave where our lantern set the thin pillars revolving like spokes of a wheel as their shadows obeyed its advancing light. The organ was away at the east end and neither of us felt quite secure somehow until we had reached it, swung back the two shutters that enclosed the manuals and lighted the candles on either side, making for us both a little lighted sanctuary of sanity and safety in the mad vast darkness of the church. Even this small safety would sometimes elude us – or at any rate Fred. Immersed in my music it was easy for me to ignore the eerie appeal of the empty echoing nave; but Fred, pumping away at the bellows had only its long intimidating shadows to concentrate upon. 'I seen somethin'' he would whisper above the notes wheezing into silence as he let the handle ride; 'I swear I 'ave.' And sometimes his fears were justified even if the intruder later turned out to be nobody more frightening than Dickie the Sexton come to stoke up the fires in the vaults under the aisle. Like other boys in the village we thoroughly disliked him since one of his duties was to keep us in order on Sundays from his face-about seat in the side aisle; he was devoted to our weekly misery but even he was welcome on organ practice nights. The clank and rattle of his iron rakers and shovels as he stoked the fires beneath, were a comforting accompaniment to my playing; and Fred released from his fears could concentrate for once on his blowing.

No doubt he earned his few coppers, for he was so small that his skinny arms as they jerked the handle up and down, appeared to be engaged in physical exercises. Understandably he soon grew tired, especially if I played with the loudest stops out and the two manuals coupled as I loved to do. For it was one of the few things I really liked about the organ in those days that it could give me such a sense of power. Played full out the rich chords throbbed through the empty church rattling the looser window panes. It was grand to be in command of so much noise and I suppose I felt very much then, as the lads of today feel astride their first motor cycle, roaming through quiet lanes. Grand for me, yes; but not for skinny Fred sweating away. 'Can't you play softer?' he would say, pitifully concerned with the excessive burden of his job. Instead of admiring the splendid noise I was making because of him, he complained! For a while, out of pity, I would use only the quieter stops – the Flute, the Stopped Diapason; but access to power is tantalizing and it was never long before I was pulling out the louder stops again – the Open Diapason, the Bassoon, the Shrill Principal – until Fred could stand it no longer and the glorious triumphant chords oozed and wheezed into silence and the wind gave out. 'I'm goin' home,' he would say, already putting both arms into his jacket and wriggling it on over his head.

Mendelssohn sonatas, especially the slow movements, came in handy as voluntaries on those rare and (to me) important occasions when I was asked to stand in for the vicar's sister who usually played the organ for Sunday services. I must have been of considerable use to her, when my proficiency had advanced far enough, for there was nobody in the village who could take over her duties when she was ill or went on holiday. Hitherto, as I can well remember, her aged brother had had to scramble his way through the services unaided, and a difficult business this was since he was not only entirely tone-deaf but had certain embarrassing awkwardnesses in the management of his teeth. Helpful as I must have been, the vicar's sister expressed no gratitude; instead she made it quite clear that the obligation was on my side, it was a privilege for a village lad to be allowed such an honour, and I was to be sure never to play any unseemly, gay or difficult music (lest I should show off, I suppose, or cast a reflection on her own inadequate talent); nor was I to drown the choir (which was hardly avoidable, anyhow, so few and feeble were they). All of which was rather damping, of course; but enough opportunity remained to make the occasions a considerable source of pride, if not of enjoyment. The organ was in full view of the congregation and I well knew, as I sat there waiting my cue from the church clock (a long crescendo wheeze culminating in the first bell of the hour), that all eyes were on me. If this was rather unnerving, it was also youthfully gratifying. My parents were there, too, watching, listening, proud of me. Well, I am glad now, as I look back, that there was at least one aspect of my musical aptitude in which they could take a harmless pride and pleasure, for in most other aspects it must have been rather a disappointment. Their appreciation of music was simple and conventional; they considered it an accomplishment, a social acquisition; and I am sure they wondered why I did not employ my musical proficiency, whether playing or singing, more willingly to this end. When visitors called, it was with reluctance that I could be persuaded to play the pieces and sing the songs they understood and admired – but at least they must have felt I was doing them credit when I played the organ for church services, and I trust this made sufficient amends.

Then the Ear
(1919–1936)

No More a Soldier

Because of continued tension in the Middle East, where I had been serving in the First World War, it was not until mid-May, 1919, that I finally arrived back in England and was given my discharge. I soon found that I had changed more than my clothes in the process: even as I sat in the train, on the journey home, it was as if a new man looked out of the carriage window at the flowering orchards and fat pastures of the Weald of Kent from which I had too long been absent.

Home for me meant the Medway valley; and I suppose that never again have I experienced anything quite so disturbingly exciting as those first days of freedom after the arid disciplines of war. In such circumstances the rediscovery of home would have been a joy at any time; but in late spring, with the woodpeckers drumming in the cherry-trees and the farm-hands striding across the hop-gardens on their lanky stilts, it was an experience that stretched the senses almost to the point of pain. The scorching Egyptian desert and the suffocating Jordan Valley – and now 'all this juice and joy' of England in Maytime! The spiritual bondage of Army life – and now this freedom to be myself and myself alone! No day could be long enough to cram into it all that I wished to do and see and hear. There were my village friends to meet again – schoolboys when I went away, young men now; and there were my favourite haunts to visit – the Hurst, the Alders, the Meadow.

I was out and about early in the morning, climbing to the Hurst to see how big my name had grown on the beech-trees where I had carved it with another's, or watching the nesting birds in the nut plantations. I dawdled all the afternoon by the stream in the Rectory copse, where the sunlight dappled the shallow water and turned the pebbles to jewels, and heard the ram thudding as if it were the earth's own heart-beat. I put down my hand among the cool bluebell stalks and the contact somehow reassured me. I listened to the men and women working in field and barn, and the rich Kentish burr of their voices comforted me. It seemed that only now was I beginning to live. This, I felt, was reality: all the rest – the training, the campaigning – was like something that had existed outside time and place: the years the locusts had eaten.

'Those who can't — teach'

I was after all a schoolmaster and should have been by now used to a
little noise. In fact, after a fashion I was even enjoying my school-
mastering: Newport was a very different matter from Bromley. The
Headmaster, Dr F.J. Wyeth, remained, as far as I was concerned, a
monacled and somewhat enigmatic figure who imposed himself as
little as possible on the school over which he none the less effectively
ruled. One sensed, rather than actively realized his presence. His
interests were nicely balanced between zoology, of which he was no
mean student, and art, which he practised with some shyness. Despite
this the school had a considerable bias towards the sciences, which
only added zest to my work as English Master, since it seemed to me
to indicate that some sort of compulsion devolved on me to try and
restore the balance.

Whether the boys, through my efforts, improved in their speech
(the day-boys, at least were mostly farmers' and small tradesmen's sons
from the locality, and their speech was always inclined to lapse back
into its Essex variant the moment the restraint of the classroom was
removed), or developed a lasting appreciation of their heritage of
literature, I would not like to say; but something they must have
gained from the hours we spent together, for even now they
occasionally come to call on me – which, since I cannot imagine myself
voluntarily calling on any of the masters who taught me at my school,
may perhaps be taken as a compliment. Furthermore, our association,
besides providing the basis for a number of friendships, has been the
means of rewarding me ever since with an annual cheque, not the less
welcome for being so exceedingly modest. It happened this way. As at
Bromley, so at Newport, my most enjoyed work with the boys

centred, not surprisingly, upon my endeavours to encourage in them a liking for English poetry. And the Newport boys, who ranged up to seventeen and eighteen, offered here an immeasurably more fertile ground than had those vociferous little cherubs from Bromley. As a result of my experience I wrote an article which was printed in *The Spectator*: whereupon, a certain publisher approached me to compile and edit *A Book of Verse for Boys* based on the methods I had outlined in my article. The consequent yearly cheque is, I am sure the boys would agree, as happy a reminder as anybody could devise of the two years we worked together.

My difficulty this time, in fact, was less with the boys than with the masters. Of that thwarted profession we must surely have been some of its oddest members. Admittedly, if one is to believe all one reads, most Masters' Common Rooms are discomforting places; yet I think ours must have excelled many of them in degree of acrimony and bitterness that could sometimes inform its conversations. In temperament we were as various as our religions which ranged from Church of England (there were two practising clergymen on the staff) and Plymouth Brethren to militant Agnosticism. Where I so often found myself in disagreement with them, however, was in the views they so vehemently expressed about the boys. They seemed expert in discovering only the worst in them. 'They ought to be put up against the wall and shot,' said one master, who had been a Major in the Army and now carried on that side in the school — though I must add that I always suspected his exceedingly martial manner of concealing a tenderness he somehow dared not trust. 'The place,' said another, 'is a sink of iniquity.' And a third master, to get his own back on the hatred that was hurled at him, like so many missiles, directly he entered a classroom, spent all his spare time peeping and prying and pouncing on his victims.

To Essex

Words and not music were increasingly my concern; I found that my writing gained a fresh impetus from the new and exciting scene and area I was busy exploring. In coming to Essex I had unwittingly discovered the type of countryside evoking my most fertile response – arable with a persisting tradition of husbandry, and a flora based both on chalk and clay. Something of the exciting strangeness I had experienced on first making the acquaintance of the Essex scene had by now passed with familiarity; but familiarity, in this case, so far from breeding contempt, bred even stronger liking. After the comparatively civilized landscape of Kent, this North-West corner of Essex, where the boulder clay gives way in places to chalk outcrops, was new and surprising. But the surprise came as much from the man-made scene as from the wild. There was something of the eighteenth century and even earlier about the look and habit of the place. The main London to Cambridge high road ran through Newport; but it was only necessary to penetrate as far as the next village, or either side of it, to be plunged into an earlier England; and even in Newport itself, the past, in some respects, was as much in evidence as the present. For one thing, the normal speech was strangely archaic. Custom, or a closer acquaintance over the years, has since altered my opinion; but when I first came to Essex, I found the dialect (akin to that which is spoken over the border in Suffolk) harsh and even boorish. In moments of excitement – a rat-hunt for example – I had no idea what the men were saying. Nor did I know then what a story of forgotten usage lay hidden in the dialect words that were still to be heard in the cottager's everyday speech. But the local speech was by no means the only reminder of the extent to which this corner of Essex had escaped the changing touch of progress. The very cottages – half-timber, with thatch and plaster – belonged to time-past; there were villages, Arkesden and Audley End, Clavering and Wendons Ambo where one seemed to have strayed into a book of old country prints. As for Thaxted, at one time the focal township of the district, it was like a place laid aside by time and forgotten. Everywhere, in fact, there were reminders of an age that had elsewhere ended with the war. Even the farm-hand's attitude towards his work was based on a land-loyalty that had become increasingly absent in other parts of the country. The farm buildings, and sometimes the farmhouses, under the effects of the growing agricultural depression, were often in a deplorable state; tumble down barns, moss on the thatch, derelict fences and weeds in the corn were the scene everywhere; and yet I was astonished at the tenacity with which in the face of increasing odds, the tradition of good, arable husbandry persisted among the farm-hands, both young and old, if not among the farmers themselves. I had not seen in Kent a similar concern on the labourer's part for the well-being of the land he must watch falling into neglect. On foot and bicycle I covered the territory closely and everywhere I found something to surprise and elate me – flails still in use for threshing beans, bush-drains in the clay, round corn-stacks on stone staddles, woven straw crowns and birds on the thatch and a hundred country observances that Kent had largely foresworn. If, hitherto, my delight in the rural scene had fed chiefly on the observation of wildlife, bird, beast and flower, now it was nourished no less on the observation of the seasonal customs and husbandries of arable farming. I was, in short, to be as interested in the cultivated scene as I had formerly been in the uncultivated. An Essex field of beans in blossom, honey-sweet and full of the purposeful buzz of bees, was now as pleasing a sight to me as a Kentish wood of bluebells.

While 'Zekiel Ploughed

'Zekiel had reached the end of a furrow. 'Woa-cam,' he said; 'woa-hup!' The two mares came to a halt. Their flanks were steaming. 'Zekiel looped the reins over the plough handle. He walked up to a bundle that lay on the hedge-grass and extracted a can of cold tea. He did everything with leisure – as a ploughman will. Ever since he could remember he had followed the plough. And now he was seventy.

'Zekiel didn't know that he was being watched. But then he never saw anything that didn't immediately concern him. A Stranger was looking at him over the hedge, his face framed in the last red sprays of the briars.

'Good-afternoon,' the Stranger said. His voice thrummed across the empty silence. 'Zekiel jumped. All through the golden afternoon his thoughts had moved endlessly round the one same task. It took time for him to project himself into this new attitude. Then, 'Good-afternoon,' he said.

One corner of the Stranger's mouth curved up, as if he were constantly about to break into a laugh. 'You've nearly come to the end of your last acre, I see. Whose fields are these?' he asked.

'Zekiel stared at the hedge. 'Yem,' he said, replying to the first question first; and then, 'Farmer Spriggs'!' There was silence. Nothing more, as 'Zekiel thought, seemed called for. 'A silent old fellow,' the Stranger said to himself.

One of the mares was restive. 'Woa, Lady,' said 'Zekiel.

'So you call that grey mare Lady, do you?' the Stranger asked.

Again 'Zekiel saw no need for comment. 'Yem,' was all he said.

'Damn the man,' the Stranger thought. 'Is he never going to say anything of his own accord?' 'Zekiel was standing on the edge of a furrow. The earth was sweating in the sun. The Stranger made one last effort. 'And what would Mr Spriggs say, I wonder, if he knew that I was keeping you here, like this, wasting his time?'

'Zekiel's blue eyes brightened. He had caught the whole drift of that remark anyway. He knew very well what Farmer Spriggs would say. His smile broadened. He opened his mouth. He laughed softly. 'Yem,' he said.

'What a fool!' the Stranger thought. 'A bachelor, I should imagine. Lives all alone. Never speaks to a soul.' Then a playful idea occurred to him. His mouth twitched. He would have a joke with the old man.

'What would you do,' he asked, very seriously, leaning his face out over the hedge, 'what would you do if, when you got home to-night, you found your cottage gone, clean gone? Not a trace of it to be seen anywhere? Nothing but the grass where it used to stand?' He paused a moment. 'Eh, what'd you do?'

He didn't wait for an answer. Stepping down from the bank, he gave 'Zekiel Good-day, and passed up the road.

'Zekiel stared after him. 'A rummy chap that,' he thought. Then he spoke softly to himself. 'Whatever do he mean, I wonder, about finding my old cottage gone? What do he mean?'

The Stranger, it happened, was quite right. 'Zekiel was a bachelor. He did live alone in a cottage. And since his cottage stood on the edge of the Common, a mile beyond Little Ledham, he hardly did see anyone to speak to. Ever since his old mother had died, he had lived alone there; and that was twenty years ago. Twenty years of loneliness. No wonder 'Zekiel hadn't much to say when strangers came popping their heads over the hedge like that, making him jump, and asking silly questions.

Ledham itself was a quiet place. In fact, they had a queer saying over at Stringer's End, the next village. They said the Lord had made their village last of all places on the earth, and that He had shovelled the dirt over on to Ledham. But 'Zekiel's cottage was in a lonelier place still.

'Zekiel, however, didn't mind loneliness. He loved his little thatched cottage – if he could be said to love anything. He was so old. His one fear was the rheumatism. Farmer Spriggs wouldn't want him as ploughman then. There would be nothing left for him then but the Workhouse.

But lonely? It was whispered down in the village that poor old 'Zekiel was a little daft, you know; only they said it kindly, because they thought him such a harmless, gentle soul. And such a lonely, forsaken life he led. But they didn't know.

There were two rooms in 'Zekiel's cottage, and a lean-to. The thatch was green with moss and grass. The sparrows bickered all day there, under the eaves. There was no garden in the front, nor much behind; but it was enough for 'Zekiel's potatoes; and his few fowls had all the Common to roam.

'Zekiel used to talk to his clock and his lamp and his bits of crockery, as any other man would talk to his dog. All the place was familiar to him, and very friendly. Twenty years of mute companionship had made even the meanest things sentient for him and kindly . . . .

So when the Stranger was gone, old 'Zekiel went about his ploughing, greatly troubled in his weak, warped mind. What was that he had said? 'What would you do if you found your cottage clean gone, and nothing but the grass where it stood?' He turned the thought over and over, never letting it rest. Darkly, and for the first time in his life, he knew that he liked his little crooked home. His blue eyes were clouded and serious.

Putting his hand to the plough again, he worked on mechanically, letting the horses have their will. He climbed the hill and passed out of sight. When he was gone there was no noise at all but a robin chirping out his tiny brass notes by the hedge. 'Zekiel came over the crest again. He looked as though every thought was bent on cutting a clean straight furrow; but a cruel maggot was eating at his brain. He was muttering to himself, 'I wonder what he do mean? . . . my cottage gone . . . only the grass?'

The afternoon wore on. The low rays of the sun burned the elms to tawny flames. Now and then a shower of yellow leaves fell, as their time came.

Strange little memories thrust themselves up into 'Zekiel's consciousness: of the way he would sit by the hearth when the wind blew round his cottage; or of the kettle singing ready for his morning tea; or of the friendly look it all had when, candle in hand, he turned the key in the door and made ready for bed. 'Gone . . . clean gone!' The foolish words went ringing on. He turned the last furrow and unharnessed the mares from the plough. He had not heard the clock strike four, some time ago.

It was already past sunset when 'Zekiel shut the gate of the farmyard behind him and turned down the lane, homewards. He had to pass through the village and across the Common. He walked with his head bent down. He saw nothing. Now and then he would pass some one; but he didn't hear their greeting. 'Poor old 'Zekiel,' they thought, 'up in the clouds, as usual!' He meant to have bought some bread in Ledham, but he quite forgot it. The words in his brain kept time with the slow clop-clop of his tread. 'Gone . . . clean gone!'

The last house of Ledham was behind him now. Not that he noticed where he was. He knew every inch of the way and could, he would have sworn, have walked it blindfolded. Indeed, he was as good as blindfolded now, so occupied was he. His mazy mind was as grey and eerie as the dusk that spread rapidly round him.

He set foot on the Common. Little threads of paths wound in all directions, in and out of the gorse and the bushes, leading this way and that. He knew them all by heart. For nearly seventy years he had trod them. Without intending to do so, he was hurrying more and more now, as he came nearer the cottage. His heart beat quickly, stabbing him with little angry pains; but he didn't notice them. Another quarter of a mile and he would be home. He plodded on. . . . 'Nothing but the grass; nothing but the grass,' his thoughts were singing.

Instinctively he knew that he must be within sight of the cottage. His eyes cleared a little. He looked up.

There was nothing there to see, in the thickening twilight, but the grey stretch of grassy Common. Then it was true? His cottage *was* gone? Clean gone!

He shut his eyes and then, half believing that he had been wrong, opened them again. No, there was nothing there. Nevertheless, he walked across the bare place, as if to make sure. Nothing was there, but grass and a bush of gorse . . . . So this was what the Stranger had meant? 'Zekiel stood still, holding his hand against his thumping heart. Did he think that, if he were only to wait long enough, the little house would return again, with all its familiar kindly sense of home? The clock, the jug, the broken stool, and the fireplace? Nothing returned.

Then suddenly he ran, stumbling, over the Common, in the direction of Little Ledham. 'Gone . . . clean gone,' he shouted wheezily.

They led him into Sarah Gee's cottage, near the smithy. He dropped into the first empty chair. He could only breathe with difficulty. They could make no sense at all, at first, of the few words he mumbled. They thought he was gone quite mad this time. And then Sarah, fancying he said something about his cottage being gone, supposed there had been a fire, and sent her boy Tommy to the Common to see.

'Zekiel was silent. His face creased up with every breath he took; and then all his muscles seemed to grow stiff. They lifted him over on to the couch. He lay quite still. Blood trickled from the corner of his mouth.

Presently Tommy came running in. 'The place bean't burnt at all, mother,' he said. It was obvious that he was disappointed there had been no fire. He appealed to another boy standing in the doorway. 'We did see it with our own eyes, didn't we, John?' Then he noticed 'Zekiel lying stiff upon the couch. 'And what be the matter with the owd man?' he asked.

The Stricken Peasant

Dim twilight here; and in her singing mind
Dim twilight too. Shut in this darkened room,
Over whose broad-beamed walls the shadows bloom,
All day she lies;
Yet will her sweet thoughts find
Nothing but praise to tell until she dies.

No footstep passes but she knows the tread;
And each some pastoral-memory awakes
Within her dreamy head.
Or when the barley-wains
Go rumbling past, darkly her old brain tells
Of other wagons jolting up the lanes
In days long since; then breaks
A tear from shrunken lids the while she dwells
On far-off romping harvests that she knew
When Ned and she to their shy loving drew.

Sometimes, for hours, no company she knows
But chattering birds
That rustle in her eaves, when the wind blows
Sparrows and starlings, jostling, helter-skelter,
To the thatch for shelter:
Yet are their pipings plain to her as words.
Or she will turn to the window's leaded panes –
On loved scenes lingering long;
And whether sun makes bright the land, or rains

THE STRICKEN PEASANT

Close it in tremulous veils, one song
Is ever at her lips – though mutely thrown
To the still air – of love and love alone.
And when the twilight fades and wagons come
Wheeling their yellow lights about her room,
As to the farm they pass along
Their very creaking is an evensong.

So with their circumstance, the days
Draw to a close; the nights dark vigil keep –
Unblessed of sleep:
Yet is her every word a meed of praise.

Such peace is hers, no knowledge gives,
Who, to no other end than loving, lives:
Such faith, no knowledge now can try,
With urgent Wherefore, Why,
To dim the brightness of her old belief.
Out of her very grief
Has grown this rich content,
Easing her soul in its lone banishment.

And often, in her dreams, the skies are riven
With a great light; till her accustomed eyes
Behold the blaze of heaven.
Upon her ears a singing breaks; the skies
Fold back and ever back; and flaxen-fair
The angels are, moving in beauty there.
The memory is so bright for her
That waking, still she fears to stir
Lest this her room and these her hands should be
A borrowed dream out of Eternity.

Two Country Parsons

Widdington in Essex, where I lived in the early twenties, was one of the places where change came slowly. It was a village with an entrance but no exit: it led nowhere. It was two miles from the nearest main road. Its four hundred inhabitants moved always a pace or two behind their neighbours and obviously liked it better that way.

Squiredom in the village had somehow disappeared, which was perhaps surprising; but the community nevertheless achieved a unity, a coherence, more reminiscent of the eighteenth than of the twentieth century. The force round which the village held was the Revd James Court, almost as much by virtue of his common humanity as of his position as rector. I had known him at Newport Grammar School near by, where he taught Latin to the senior boys and scripture to the juniors. Nobody, and least of all himself, would have claimed that he was a scholar; nor was he a disciplinarian. We all knew, from the laughter and shouting that came through the open windows, when Jimmy (as he was affectionately called) was in class. But the laughter was good-tempered and the shouting mere animal spirits: both master and boys were enjoying themselves.

If Jimmy lacked discipline when he wore his gown in the classroom, he lacked it no less when he wore his surplice in church; but the same qualities that triumphed over his disadvantage in the one place served no less in the other. He was of the type, saint as jester. Coming up the aisle from the vestry at morning service, he would tack a little off course to say to one of the congregation, 'Nine across, six letters. What is it?' For the crossword puzzle was coming into fashion and Jimmy was an addict. His sermons lacked any sort of shape; they rambled; their sense, like their sentences, got tied up in knots; but they were comfortably short, and they spoke from the heart to the heart.

The village school was his, no less than the church. It was indeed one of the last church schools to remain so in more than name. Over the door, carved in a slab of stone, were the words, 'Behold, I will teach you the fear of the Lord.' But in fact, fear, if not of the Lord, certainly of his emissary, was the last emotion its scholars experienced. Every morning Jimmy would run across from the rectory to give a token scripture lesson before hurrying back to finish his breakfast and then race his rackety open car down to Newport, late as usual for the first Latin period.

I think he put more work into the village brass band than into any other of his activities. It was his pride and joy. In winter the weekly band practices were held in the school and in summer on the green; but summer or winter, indoors or out, the noise was equally penetrating. Even Newport heard it if the wind was in the right quarter; and Widdington itself compulsorily stopped paying attention to anything else. Louder than the brass was Jimmy's own voice as he bawled his injunctions to the performers. He knew little about music, as he cheerfully admitted, but somehow he managed to get fair results: at any rate, it was not only because there was no other brass band in the vicinity that Widdington's was in considerable demand for summer fêtes and flower shows, where, in handed-down uniforms and with mugs of beer at their feet, the men blew their loudest and best.

There was indeed an idyllic quality about Widdington in those days, despite the economic and political unrest so painfully evident elsewhere in the country. We may even have been too unaware of what was going on: Jarrow seemed so very far away. Any lack of social consciousness on our part, however, was perhaps made up for by the zeal displayed in this direction at Thaxted near by.

An old green bridle-path led through the fields from Widdington to Thaxted, or at least to Cutlers Green, where the Guild of Cutlers had established a settlement in the days when Thaxted was the Sheffield of the south. The track extended for three or so miles and was an excellent place for walking; and since any walk is the better for having an aim in view I was often attracted that way, knowing that at the end of it there awaited me a work of art, for that is very much what the services in Thaxted church meant for me. Although the ceremonial depended largely on the inhabitants, many of them farm-hands, it could achieve a beauty, even a grandeur, not often found in country churches.

If Conrad Noel was not himself an artist, he gathered artists about him; and a better place in which to exercise their skills could hardly be imagined than this great church, where the pews had been taken out and the plain glass windows let in the day. Even the flowers set at effective points of vantage declared the artist's hand; so did the furniture and trappings. Cool blowing green curtains, like spring rain, shut off the two side chapels, and bright banners hung above the chancel. The music, too, was invariably fine, especially on festive occasions when, under the guidance of Gustav Holst, it provided a pleasure too rarely associated with country life.

For this I was grateful – as who could not be? – to the man who had inspired it; but gratitude was not what he wanted. Time and again Conrad Noel would point the moral that the Thaxted services were meant to be a communal effort; yet I felt that I was by no means the only one in the congregation who had come, as it were, to see the sights. If the coloured ceremonials sometimes lulled me like an opiate, especially on such occasions as the eve of Corpus Christi when the chapel glowed like a ruby in the otherwise darkened church, I never lost grip on myself. The Thaxted Movement, in short, was something to which I could not lend a total sympathy, nor yet could I keep away from it. I respected it, because I respected the man round whom it centred; and I enjoyed it, at least in part, because it made such fine use of the arts; but I did not want to probe deeper.

To see Conrad Noel enter the church before service, clanking the great iron latch of the south door behind him, was to have no conception of the man who would presently enslave us all with his words. Doffing his biretta, he bobbed perfunctorily to the altar and shuffled off to the vestry. To any lesser man his hare-lip alone might have been a handicap; but no sooner had he climbed into the pulpit and delivered his text than the deformity was forgotten in the power of his presence and in the force and originality of what he said. There was bite in his words and he emphasized it with a sort of snarl. He would rouse his congregation to open laughter; and then, before the creases were out of their faces, he would turn the joke upon them. He had learning and pressed it vigorously into his interpretation of the Gospels, to which he gave a contemporary, not to say socialist, slant.

Listening to him, we were not likely to forget our personal share in the general responsibility for the poverty, unemployment, frustration and uneasy peace of the twenties. He made the story of Christ touch our own lives at every point.

Yet in the Thaxted Movement itself there seemed to me to be more than a hint of sensationalism. At any rate some of its members contrived to give me the impression that they were spoiling for a fight; and when the so-called Battle of the Flags was duly joined, their attitude rather suggested that this was just what they had been waiting for. The flags in question were the Sinn Fein tricolour and the Red Flag, both of which, as a matter of fact, had been hanging in the church with other flags and banners throughout the war without arousing opposition. It was not until Thaxted incensed certain sections of the public by openly espousing the cause of the locked-out miners in 1921 that the flags had become a point of controversy. Lorry-loads of angry oppositionists drove over from Cambridge (the opposition never came much from Thaxted itself) and tore down the flags. No sooner were they replaced than they were torn down again. Presently the raiders came from as far afield as Chatham. Sleepy little Thaxted woke up with a shock to find itself the centre of rowdy scenes that were prominently featured in the national press.

Essex cottagers are perhaps even cannier than most and so, whatever their private thoughts on the matter may have been, the general run of the Thaxted population took little active part in the fight. This they left to the avowed crusaders under the leadership of Father Bucknell who had come to Thaxted from the East End of London, and whose sense of the drama of events was such that (so it was said) he talked on one occasion of concealing himself in a priest's hiding-hole in an old farmhouse near by if the need should arise. In fact it was all very thrilling if not, for me at least, quite convincing.

After the rather feverish atmosphere of Thaxted it was a relief to return to the simple sanities of Widdington. 'Where have you been?' Jimmy Court would ask, knowing quite well where I had been. 'A-whoring after strange gods?' It would have been useless to discuss such matters with him. He governed his life by rules based on an almost childlike simplification of the word of Christ. He knew his limitations; and what he did not understand he did not venture to meddle with. His tiny backwater parish was his sufficient world and he ruled it like a father his family. Considering the state of the country at the time, this may seem to have been unwarrantably escapist: the point is that it worked. Widdington may have been backward as far as social responsibilities were concerned: I only know that it radiated contentment.

Frank Kendon in Cambridge

We grow as much by our friends, during the years of early manhood, as by our own endeavours or by the influence of our surroundings, whether self-chosen or imposed. Certainly this was so in my case. I was fortunate in the place where I was born, in Kent – Cobbett's 'finest seven miles I have ever seen in England, or anywhere else'; and fortunate in the place where I came to work, in North West Essex. But above all I think I was fortunate in my friends of that period. They were possessed of true individuality and many of them were creators, makers. The maker is the giver; and to be his friend is continually to receive grace from that abundance with which he surrounds himself. His friendship is a warm spring air in which one's bare boughs bud and thrive, a nourishing soil in which one's searching roots find food. I am especially reminded of this in respect of one of my friends, Frank Kendon, the poet. I have enjoyed his friendship for over thirty years and never more fruitfully I suppose than in the time immediately following the war. We both came from Kent, yet I might never have met him if he had not chanced on me one day in an Embarkation Camp outside Marseilles where I was sitting on a rolled-up blanket in the sand before my tent, reading from a copy of Palgrave's *Golden Treasury*. We embarked on the same troopship for Egypt, sleeping on the crowded decks by night (to wake smothered with dew and with soot from the ship's funnels), and playing chess against the railings by day on a pocket set which Kendon carried in his kit. But it was not until after the war that we found in our common interest in poetry and pictures, that communion of fellowship to which I at least owe so much. He was up at Cambridge, where he had succeeded in gaining admission to St John's College, by an early application which had had a luckier reception than my own; and Cambridge was within easy cycling distance of Newport.

Kendon stayed up for part of that summer vacation and I lodged awhile on his hospitality in order to spend with him such time as he could spare from his studies. He had taken over a friend's rooms in college, whose barred window looked over the River Cam where it flows under the Bridge of Sighs. Punts and canoes drifted below the window and the voices of their occupants, held by the walled-in water, sounded close and clear. The weeping golden willows dipped their long fingers in the river, making ripples like rising fish, and from the tennis courts came the quick smack of ball on racket. It was youth's summertime. Such students as had not gone down for the vacation lay sprawled out on the lawns, their books open before them. I sensed then at least the savour of what I had missed in not being able to come up to Cambridge as an undergraduate. And yet, outsider though I was now, enjoying by chance a peep into the 'what might have been', I was nevertheless far too happy for regrets. We biked up the river as far as the No Hurry Inn ('Five Miles from anywhere') alongside the water, experiencing thereby a new level of vision, almost a new world – where voles dived into the water and disappeared, and wild duck flew up from the rushes and purple spires lived again in their larger than life reflections. The muddy smell of water was with us all the way. Or we walked along the tow-path from the colleges, to Grantchester, not yet smothered in fame, and dreamed as we leant over the weir; or to Madingley, where the nightingales sang at noon and heedless of the traffic of the main road nearby. Or we sat in Kendon's window-seat above the water, whose waves dappled the stone bridge with dancing sun-spots, and read turn and turn about from Shakespeare and Chaucer, Blake and (though this seems somehow incongruous) Conrad. Or, while Kendon was busy, in the library or attending a lecture, I dawdled about the colleges, delighted with everything but far and away the most of all by King's Chapel. Not the Mosque of Omar in Jerusalem had stirred my spirit as this marvel of architecture now did – and has done ever since – soaring into the sky, so outrageously incongruous in its conception, so finally congruous in its effect. I sat in the polished oak pews of the nave, bemused by the gathered grace of the centuries, while the blue stained light fell in shafts across the floor and the griffons pranced among the Tudor roses. Acceptance over the years has never dimmed the pleasure King's Chapel can give, so that to enter is still and immediately to experience a quietening both of sense and spirit; but in those days of my first acquaintance with it, the effect was akin to hearing Beethoven's Ninth Symphony or seeing Da Vinci's *Virgin of the Rocks* – a proof in solid stone, it seemed, of that divine exultation to which man rarely and by mercy may aspire.

Such a prolonged spell of Kendon's company was, however, exceptional. We met from time to time, but friendship was fed, no less, by many letters wherein we shared our delight in art and our countryman's pleasure in nature. Perhaps his letters, and mine also, in a measure were the means we employed (though not consciously, of course) to explore and integrate our discoveries by putting them down on paper – there is nothing like a good listener for clarifying one's thoughts. In helping me, in fact, Kendon was helping himself – at any rate I hope he was for the news and views included in my own letters could have been no sort of adequate recompense for the maturity of judgment and delicacy of perception expressed in his. We often included our latest poems (as well as examples of our latest finds among others' poems) in our letters; and here Kendon was always the one audience I wished to please. But he was hard to satisfy. Of some poems I had sent him, he complained, I remember, that they did not trust sufficiently to the constructive conception of the reader: 'If you give a stark idea,' he wrote, 'you ought to rest content that the reader would have the decency enough to clothe it.' Of others he said: 'They give me the horrid feeling of hot hands – a little too close you were to the subject.' I was enamoured of words, and such advice, salutary as I recognized it to be, was not easy to follow: the adjective and the adverb continued to snare me.

Sir John Reith

It was in August or September 1928 that I had the chance of an interview for work with the BBC. The interview was timed for two-thirty at Savoy Hill and in my nervousness I presented myself earlier than I need have done, but the reception clerk straightway handed me over to a brisk, braided attendant who conducted me to the ante-room of Sir John Reith's office. A spectacled secretary, discreet and obviously efficient, strode silently over the pile carpet to greet me: 'Sir John won't be long,' she said, handing me a magazine to pass the time and immediately disappearing. The clock ticked in the high austere room, inexorably reckoning each minute's discomfort. Then, at two minutes past the half-hour the outer door opened and through my pretended absorption in the magazine on my lap, I saw his two long pin-striped legs eat up the distance to the door of the office. I dared to glance up just in time to see Sir John's immensely tall and commanding figure pause a moment at the door while he searched me with a penetrating eye. I was alone again in the awful silence. Suddenly the sheer idiocy of my quest overwhelmed me. What on earth was I doing here? By what incredible misappliance of good fortune had I obtained this interview that was about to be vouchsafed me? If I could have slunk away I think I surely would have done so then. But the inner door opened and there was Sir John himself beckoning me. 'Come along,' he said, checking his wrist watch by the clock. 'I see I'm late. I'm not usually late.' He closed the door behind us, sat down at an enormous desk and then indicated a chair for me, immediately before him.

Unused as I was, from my country breeding and the kind of life I had led, to the customs and techniques of Big Business, I did not realize at the time that what I was experiencing now was only the routine procedure of any high-powered executive. To Sir John, of course, this was just another interview – one of hundreds which he conducted in the course of his duties as Director-General of the most talked-of new business venture in Britain – and all, no doubt, in much the same manner, with much the same (shall I say) tricks of the trade. To me, however, it was nothing so usual. In my innocence (some might say ignorance) I had no idea that I was being the victim of tricks, or that the interview was anything but a genuine attempt (which of course it also was) to probe my ability and assess its value, if any, to the Corporation. It was only considerably later, when my service in the BBC had somewhat sharpened my wits and initiated me a little into the ways of a decidedly unidealistic world, that I realized this was all part of an act which Sir John knew by heart and had the total mastery of.

Even the lighting was artfully arranged. My chair had been so placed that the sun, concentrated in the window behind Sir John's desk, shone full on me, like a searching (and to me most discomforting) spot-light. And further to give himself the initial advantage, my interviewer said nothing, but, immediately upon taking his seat, put the telephone receiver to his ear and conducted what may well have been an unnecessary conversation – unnecessary that is to say, except in that it gave him time to take a long look at me and assess in advance what manner of person I might be. This done, and my discomfort having put me at his mercy, he began his questions, all of which were totally unlike anything I might reasonably have anticipated and one of which could perhaps only have come from this stern son of a Scottish manse. 'What,' he asked, in a sonorous voice that marvellously triumphed over what sounded like a mouthful of plum, 'what do you make of Jesus Christ in the world of today?' In all honesty I wish I could remember my answer to this poser, but I cannot – the shock of the question itself apparently drove it out of my mind. Yet, as I was to learn later, this was exactly the sort of question Sir John would ask. He was a dourly religious man and obviously believed in harnessing his religion to the needs of every day.

I find, on looking back to that momentous interview, that few indeed of the answers I gave have stuck in my memory. What could I possibly have found to say, for instance, when Sir John asked: 'If something had given rise to friction between the BBC and one of the Government departments, and you were sent to smooth matters over, how would you set about it?' Such a contingency, or anything like it, had never come within miles of my narrow experience, yet I must have mumbled out some sort of answer, and as was presently to transpire, it could not have been so desperately wide of the mark as to put me quite out of the reckoning. Either mother's wit must have been unusually kind to me just then or I possess a fund of intuitive wisdom which I should certainly make more use of than I do. When I supposed the interrogation had at last come to an end, Sir John surprised me by suddenly adopting a confidential, even avuncular, tone and saying, 'We can speak as man to man here and I'm going to ask you a very personal question. I understand that you never attended a Public School. Now tell me; do you experience any sense of, shall we say, inferiority when you come into contact with men who have had the advantage of a Public School education?' To this question I do recall my answer: 'None at all,' I said. Whereupon Sir John picked up the phone and I heard him say, 'I have somebody here who has been sent to me by Geoffrey Dawson. Anybody who interests the Editor of *The Times* interests me. Have you a place for him somewhere? I don't want you to make a place for him but if there is one, I think he should have it.' I supposed the interview was now really at an end and accordingly I rose to take leave of the presence. But there was apparently one more point to be made. 'If you should decide to join us, as I hope you will,' said Sir John, 'remember that the BBC does not want you only for so many hours a day; it wants you body and soul.'

Goodnight Vienna

Sir John, it was soon clear to me, had chosen his underlings with an imaginative foresight, a wisdom, not usually credited to this austere figure in those days. In building up his organization, he had not forgotten the necessity for men of creative, as well as executive, talent – some would even say he favoured the creative element too much; but I do not agree. It was customary, for example, to smile tolerantly at the goings-on of Lancelot de Gibenne Sieveking (to give Lance Sieveking his full name, savouring as it does of Icelandic saga and Arthurian legend and Norman knights). Radio was a gargantuan toy for him and radio drama the game he played with it. Seated at the control panel (a new invention just then) he manipulated it like a Wurlitzer organ, cutting out one studio and cutting in another, fading out this music and fading in that, till it seemed the whole building must be full of studios which, as the whim of his genius dictated, he called upon to produce his kaleidoscopic effect, wherein anything might be let loose on the listeners, from mowing machines to mewing cats, screaming women to sea-gulls. Yet out of this fantastic melée, more sound effects than drama, a new radio form was born which all radio dramatists ever since owe a debt to.

Eric Maschwitz too, the Editor of *The Radio Times*, was in his own way, no less typical of this high-spirited band of young enthusiasts. As his assistant I shared a desk with him in a vast room that was as full of continual comings and goings as a railway terminus. He was as far removed from Brailsford, my only other editorial contact so far, as Bing Crosby from Bach; but he was exactly the man for the job. Nervous, enormously energetic, as lively as a fish in a net, quick and dashing as mercury, he proved more than equal to the hundred and one emergencies that were inherent in the daily round. Lacking entirely as yet the split-second efficiency that must inevitably characterize so vast an organization as the BBC has since become, I was amazed then, as I am amazed still, that we were able, under his darting bright eye, to produce each week with so few mistakes a paper that had to cater impartially for the many conflicting programme departments and present in an easily readable fashion the vast and chaotic array of programmes they daily presented us with. And yet even so absorbing a job could not, apparently, exhaust his tireless energy. During the time I worked with him I should say that, without for an instant slacking his hold on his BBC work or dwindling a jot in his enthusiasm and contribution to the new medium of sound radio, he must have devoted as many hours (he seemed to stay up half the night) and as much purposeful activity to writing romantic song lyrics and ingenious (and invariably romantic) playlets and sketches for various theatrical ventures as would have seemed of themselves to constitute a whole-time occupation. We shared an inter-communicating telephone and in time I grew quite used to the colourful variations this could provide to my routine work. Clapping a hand over the mouthpiece of his phone, into which he had been speaking with one of his several composers, Eric would say, 'Pick up your receiver a moment,' and I would hear at the other end of the line somebody trying over on the piano the music for one of his latest lyrics. It was in this manner that I had the privilege (not to put too fine a point on it) of being in at the birth of that popular ditty of Eric's 'Goodnight Vienna', with George Posford fumbling over the notes of the tune that had just come to him (so he announced) in his bath. This lyric like all the writing Eric did 'on the side' was written over the name of Holt Marvell, and I was never quite sure who it was sitting opposite me at the desk, Eric the editor or Holt the song and sketch writer.

Arrival in Provence

The dusty autobus crawled up the last hundred yards of the hill and then, as if to give its occupants a moment in which to recover from the shock of so sudden and magnificent a view, slackened almost to a standstill on the crest. For well over an hour, slowly it had wormed its way through the gloom of the gorges; and there had been little enough to prove the fact that the hour was early afternoon, the place Provence, and the month September. But now, with an abruptness that hurt the eyes, the chilly gloom of the tunnelling rocks had given place to a burning, golden air and the sky had dropped to touch the full round of a green horizon. After all those barren miles, where only the deluding beauty of a pounding river, far below, had given life to the rocky landscape, there was something fantastic, flamboyant, about the strident green valley that now came into view. The wide fields were lit with the tall, erect flames of poplar trees; here and there a farmhouse, protected from the blaze of the sun by a feathery cluster of acacias, gave point to the intense fertility; and the river that had recently foamed and thundered through dark caverns, could be seen flashing and curling in and out of the lush meadows.

Not that many of the people in the 'bus seemed to be noticing these things: to most of them they were all as familiar, as expected, as their own sunburned hands. But to Christopher Severn and his wife, Marie, this sudden, green prospect was like the first glimpse of a Promised Land. Christopher, the better to get his bearings, leaned out of the window. The sunlight fell with almost unbearable heat upon his pale skin; but he cherished the pain of it and was glad. Presently, he pointed to a small, white village that gleamed in the light and seemed to be hanging on to the face of an outcrop of hills in the distance.

'That's Beauvoir,' he said to Marie; 'I feel sure it is.'

There was nothing in the tone of his voice to suggest how much it meant to him to be able to make that simple assertion at last; but Marie understood.

Christopher turned to ask a man on the opposite seat if he was right; but even as he leaned over the gangway, excitedly the man began to speak to his friends. Christopher was ignored. The man's eyes were blue as speedwell flowers and very bright: there was an unusual dignity about the quick, spare features of his peasant face. And now he was busy telling some tale or other, though what it was all about Christopher had no idea; for one thing the 'bus was rattling downhill and making a great clatter and for another Christopher was not at all familiar with the local patois. But it did not matter: the man was so eloquent with his hands that it was almost possible to make out his meaning by them alone. Christopher watched, quite forgetful of the question he had been going to ask. What intensity the man could put into the nervous movement of those grimy hands! They fluttered like wings; they mimicked; they emphasized every high light of the story, giving it speed, giving it rhythm. By their aid, Christopher tried to discover what the story was about. Yes, it was a murder. Away down there the body had been found. . . . But no, it was a marriage. He could almost fancy he heard the crack of whips, the flickering of laughter. . . . And then again, it was neither. It was – but he gave up wondering what it was. Why worry? Clearly, this was the best of all tales that were ever told and this man was the very genius of all troubadours. Still the tale went on, and Christopher remained in thrall of those speaking hands. Then, suddenly, the voice of Marie drew him out of his dream.

'Then we shall soon be there?' she asked; and it was only with an effort of will that Christopher grasped the sense of what she had said.

But Marie too was in a sort of dream. Ever since she had first met Christopher – more than three years ago – the name of Beauvoir had been familiar to her. He was always talking about the place. She had no very clear picture of it in her mind; but she knew that to Christopher, even as a boy, it had meant some desirable haven to which he would ultimately attain. And it had been just the same with him ever since he had gone to work among those spruce, sophisticated young men and women at the Commodore Gramophone Studios. One day – how often she had heard him declare it! – he would shake free from all this humbug, this death-in-life, this useless round of activity among the whims of temperamental prima donnas and the half-baked propositions of windy-headed Directors.

'Ugh!' he would rage. 'I'd like to go and live with people who don't even know what a gramophone record looks like – let alone the fools who make 'em.'

And if Marie suggested that such people might be hard to find these days, he would only rage the more at having his words construed so literally.

'Anyway,' he would add, calmed at the sight of her appealing face, childlike and gathering to just the slightest pucker, 'when I get my holiday this autumn, we're going to Beauvoir; and if there are any gramophones there, I'll smash them to pieces.'

Beauvoir, always Beauvoir! As if the place had some mysterious hold on him, some significance for him which she could never rightly understand. Almost an obsession! So then Marie would laugh, pat him on the head, and tell him he had Beauvoir on the brain.

'No, not on the brain,' he would answer; 'but in my blood, Marie.'

And that was true enough. He had been born in Beauvoir. Not that he could remember anything tangible about it: he was only a year old when his parents had been compelled to return to England. His father's business (as all his friends had been careful to remind him) had toppled into ruin through mismanagement. 'You can't live in Provence,' they said, 'and expect to be able to look after your business in London.' And that, so far as the Severn family was concerned, had been the end of Beauvoir. Nevertheless, Christopher continued to look on it as his rightful home; and though he loved England well enough, there was always something of the exile in him. In Beauvoir he had been born and to Beauvoir he would return. He knew he would return: he must. Deep inside him the knowledge burned. The fact that he must also earn a living for himself and Marie – and later on, he supposed, for a family – was not something to be reckoned with in this mood. Everybody assured him that his job was a good one and that, in these days, he was exceptionally lucky to have secured it; but that did not prevent Christopher from thinking otherwise. Of course, as jobs go, it was good; but all jobs were a slavery, and he did not relish being anybody's slave: that was his simple view of the matter. Gramophones might give him his daily bread; but that was no earthly reason why, in return, he should be expected to give them his soul. He watched the other men and women at the Studios, as they went about their work, and he knew that their brisk cynicism was only a blind for their inner disgust: in some cases he could even see how their sensitiveness was slowly withering and all their spirit's vividness fading before the hated necessity of a deadening routine. And he vowed to himself that, if he could possibly help it, he would never allow himself to suffer a similar fate. The grip of circumstances – yes, that was what it was: those people were all in the grip of circumstances. He looked round among his friends. It was the same tale everywhere – only sometimes the submission was willingly made and sometimes it was stubbornly resisted for a few years. But for himself, there was still a freshness in him and almost anything seemed possible. Married less than a year, he seemed only just to have embarked upon life. He would never submit to slavery: somewhat naively he took this for his creed. And always at the back of his mind, to help him, there was this dream of Beauvoir.

And now the little village itself was actually in sight, small and bright in the distance, as they stared at it from the rackety old 'bus, a bunch of blazing walls at the foot of the steep rocks, tiny and indistinct, but not the less Beauvoir for that. The troubadour, his story ended, had said it was: in half an hour they would arrive. Marie's eyes were lighted with the joy of her anticipation.

The whole journey, in fact, had been a crescendo of anticipation for her. She had never set foot out of England before. They had left London in a grey, September rain. All the way across the north of France the rain had continued; and it was still raining when they pulled down the carriage-blinds to try to get some sleep. Dijon had been a dreary tumult of shuntings and shrill whistlings, and then, an hour or so from Arles, they had thrown open the windows on a new and gleamingly hot world. Provence had begun: the dream had at last budded into fact. But even then it had seemed as if Christopher could hardly believe it. He had remained shut within himself, and for most of the journey down to the coast he had spoken little: as if he were stunned by the sheer radiance of the world in which he now found himself. Marie watched him, as he stared silently out of the window at the olive-trees that were planted almost to the edge of the sea – a sea fierce in its blueness – and the warmth of her love for him was like a faintness on her; so that, if it had not been for the presence in the compartment of some highly respectable Frenchwomen on their way to the Riviera, she would have kissed him as she longed to do.

Then had come Marseilles. They stepped out into a city of sights and smells so alien that it seemed to her she must have travelled half-way across the world already. They rested at an hotel for the night; and when, at six o'clock the next morning, they climbed the wide, stately flight of steps up to the station, Marie saw something which finally stamped the South upon her brain. Mounting the white steps in front of them, slowly and sedately, while the morning sun threw long, spikey shadows from the overhanging palms, was a courtly Moroccan. He had on a black-and-gold turban and a gaily striped burnous, and on his unstockinged feet was a pair of bright, scarlet sandals. It was those sandals, thonged over the tanned and shapely feet, that fixed Marie's attention most of all. She could not forget the tall Moroccan; and when, later in the morning, they once more left the train and clambered into the autobus which was to carry them the five hours' journey across country to Beauvoir, she felt quite sure that sooner or later the driver would be called to halt, a voluminous burnous would be gathered up in a dark, beringed hand, and two scarlet sandals would proudly scale the 'bus.

But no scarlet sandals had come in sight, and here they were under the walls of Beauvoir. They could see the town more exactly now. Its buildings were huddled tightly together – a cluster of blinding-bright houses that looked as if they must have been built on to the side of the bare, precipitous cliffs that climbed to the sky. It lay full in the eye of the afternoon sun, the green and blue shutters of its windows closed against the powerful rays. Backed by the towering rocks, it faced all one way, into a green and fertile valley.

The 'bus struggled noisily up the little hill into the village; and Beauvoir, which from the distance had looked so still and sleepy, proved on nearer view to be full of life – leisurely, colourful life. To Christopher and Marie it looked very friendly and inviting. Under the largest weeping-willow tree they had ever seen, some half-a-dozen women were washing clothes in a great stone trough by the side of the road; and as the 'bus passed, smothering them with floury dust, they paused in their work and called a greeting to the driver. Down a narrow side-street came a toppling load of grass, almost hiding the slow mule that was drawing it along; and a breath of sweetness and green freshness triumphed for a moment over the fumes of the petrol. In the intense shade of interiors, wheelwrights and potters were busy at their tasks. Everywhere there were signs of quiet, purposeful activity. To Marie it was all still rather like a picture in a beautiful book: strange and brilliant and not very much to do with the realities of everyday life. But to Christopher it seemed a fit match for his dream.

Out and About

One day there arrived at the cottage John Dinkerly of the BBC and his wife Kay. I had known them when I was on the BBC staff in Manchester, but Dinkerly had just been appointed Director of the Midland Region and he and Kay would sometimes drive down from Birmingham to the cottage on a visit. On this occasion, however, it turned out to be as much a business visit as a friendly one. We had carried our tea up the meadow and were lying sprawled in the shade of the beechwood. During the conversation as we gazed out idly over the sunlit view, I chanced to tell them of a recent excursion I had made somewhere out in the wolds. I told it to share it, giving it all the details I thought necessary to bring it alive for my listeners, wanting, as it were, to take them along with me. When I had finished the tale, Dinkerly said – 'You ought to broadcast' – and then he outlined a scheme, as if it had been worked out on the inspiration of the moment, though I am convinced it was really the result of previous consideration, probably with his staff at their weekly programme conference. Or was it, perhaps that my narrative had sparked off the idea? The difficulty, he seemed to imply, was what I should broadcast. It was, in fact, my problem as a writer all over again, but transformed, this time, from the written to the spoken word. And, as it happened, the solution in the one case led to the solution in the other. 'I know what,' said Dinkerly, still seeming to improvise on the moment; 'we will send you round the region – anywhere you like to go, and you shall come to the microphone and tell listeners your experiences. We'll make a fortnightly series of it and call it *Out and About* – would you like that?' I would indeed, and agreed forthwith. It was ultimately settled that the first series should begin in October and go on throughout the winter. As it happened it went through from autumn to spring for three years; and no task I had hitherto or have since done was quite so enjoyable, or even perhaps so productive. For, by sensing what I had the ability to do, and utilizing this ability, there is no doubt that Dinkerly had been instrumental in starting me along the lines which were to develop in me to the point where I would become the kind of writer I was fundamentally best equipped to become.

To describe, so that others may seem actually to share the experience described, is what all country writers strive to do and if the writer is a poet too, his chances of succeeding are obviously enhanced. Such a task demands, apart from the actual craft of words, a seeing eye – the poet's eye that seizes at once upon the essential in whatever is before him, the characteristic feature, however shy and elusive or missed by most. Jefferies had it more perhaps than any other country writer; and Hudson had it too but often he let his theories and notions get in the way; and among modern country writers, it is the very sign-manual of the work of both Llewelyn Powys and Adrian Bell. To be numbered among this company, however lowly, would be reward enough (for all that may have been sacrificed to such an attainment). Theories change and grow out of date; most ideas have a transient life; but a clear and lucid description vital with the life of the thing described, has the marks of permanence upon it.

This is how it came about, then, that I embarked upon a Cotswold voyage of discovery that took me, over the three years of its duration, into almost every corner of those hills and far beyond. For *Out and About* was not primarily a Cotswold but a Midlands series and so I was able to extend my journeyings considerably beyond home territory. Mainly too, they were to be country rambles (I went on foot wherever possible helped out, sometimes, by trains and buses), but I could include towns if I wished to do so (I even included a tour of a well-known motor works but I doubt whether on this occasion my listeners enjoyed hearing about it any more than I had enjoyed the experience of it). In fact I was given a free hand, and to this extent the series was very much a pioneering effort in broadcasting. Nowadays when the BBC turns anybody loose on the countryside, to bring back copy, it accompanies him with recording vans and an army of engineers. This way, of course, any countryman who happens to get snatched up by the broadcasters and pushed in front of the microphone or camera is quite scared out of his natural wits and becomes at once proper material for a cheap comedy sketch. As for the broadcaster himself, his job is less to describe than to act as compere, less to present the scene to his listeners than to present himself as a broadcast personality. *Out and About* had none of today's radio aids and none of these limitations. My job was so to present the scene (or whatever it was) in my own words and only in these, that the listener should be enabled to see it through my eyes as closely, as enjoyably as I had done. That I succeeded is, I think, proved by the letters all of which more or less added up to the same thing – 'As we listened we went along with you all the way.' Those letters, handed over Allanhay's gate by our staunch (and I must confess old) postwoman, were often as revealing as they were heartening. The postlady would say, 'There's another bundle from your well-wishers this morning, Mr Warren, and I'm sure you may include me among them.' Not only did they give the task itself an added impetus, they also assured me (and I should have otherwise found it difficult to believe, in those early days of broadcasting as I sat alone in the studio reading my script) that I was speaking to people who were actually keen to hear, and who, indeed even felt they knew me. I always felt one of the greatest compliments came from someone who said they were too lazy to turn me off and then stayed enthralled. A small bus deposited me one snowy morning on Bibury bridge and after I had spoken awhile with the unknown driver, asking directions from him, he said, 'Aren't you Mr Warren? I recognized your voice.' Such instances were trivial enough in themselves but they were many.

The Countryside
in Winter

How often we hear somebody say, 'I agree that the country is beautiful enough in summer – nothing in fact could be nicer – but give me the town in winter.' The implication is that in winter the country is all mud and bareness, darkness and dreariness. When I tell London acquaintances that I live in the Cotswolds, they say, 'How lovely! We must come and look you up sometime.' And true to their word one day they arrive. 'How lucky you are!' they exclaim. But that is in summer: in winter, I notice, they seldom come near the place. The people I then meet on my walks and journeyings, and stay a moment to pass the time of day with, are people who live in the country all the year round, people who know that it is really no more empty or lonely in winter than in summer, people who understand that it takes all kinds of weather to make an English year and who relish the rain in its season just as much as they do the sun. It is only an urban conviction that however delightful the country may be in summer, in winter it is a place to be avoided.

This morning the newspapers were full of tales of blind hours in the cities, black-outs and all sorts of inconveniences – and worse. But as I look back on my own yesterday I remember it as a day of blue and silver, of brilliant patches of sunlight and shifting veils of fog; of a sun full and glorious one minute and then, the next, a great white incandescent light in the sky; of a noon as warm and beautiful as the first days of spring and of an afternoon of darkening mystery, when people came upon one suddenly out of nowhere and the trees loomed like ghosts overhead.

From Stroud I turned off up the Slad valley into a thickening fog. I hoped perhaps it would clear once I had climbed up on to the ridge, but as I pushed up the hill there was no sign of the fog lifting. Painswick, that should have been a town of bright stone, gleaming over the other side of the valley, the vane of its church spire shining like a spark and its surrounding fields green with winter pasture, was nowhere to be seen. The road was silent and deserted. Once I passed a woman driving a little pony-shay into Stroud. She nursed a child on her knee and at the same time guided the slow old pony along the road. And once, as the fog momentarily lifted, I saw a ploughman coaxing his three horses along the furrows, a lonely figure that quickly vanished into the fog again. But for the rest, all the way up from Bull's Cross, I met nobody. And then, dramatically, as I came into Miserden, the fog cleared and the sun shone out of a sky as blue as a grocer's sugar-bag. In the Carpenters' Arms I rested for a while with my feet stretched out in front of the open fire, while the landlord sat in the window-seat and talked. I asked him what he thought would be a good circular walk from here, and when he had directed me I set out again.

Entering Miserden Park, through some fine wrought iron gates, I seemed to have stepped straight into spring. Aconites bloomed under the trees, so large and plutocratic that they would have been out of place anywhere but near a mansion. The sun filtered through the overhanging boughs and turned the beech leaves on the ground into a Field of the Cloth of Gold. And yet, lovely as it all was, it was with something of relief that at last I found myself at the further gates and once more in the world outside. The friendly hedges by the roadside, the voices of men at work in a small farm nearby, the call of a strutting cockerel – these things, after 'the picturesque quiet of the park, with its avenues of trees, its lack of activity, its broad hint of the distinction of classes, all rather suggested stepping out of a picture into real life. How much more welcome seemed the happy jog-trot life in field and farm than the frigid beauty in seclusion the other side of the palings!

It was not long before I came upon a ploughman working in a field of (as I afterwards learned) twenty-two acres. Sitting on a five-barred gate I watched him steering his horses along the furrow with such ease that he made the job appear like child's-play. The field, still green with grass and sainfoin, had been cut up by guiding furrows: it was to be converted into wheat. I had already noticed, for at least half a mile along the road, that the barbed wire fencing inside the hedge was hung with tufts of wool in which the morning moisture sparkled like glass. Anybody who bothered to do so, could have gathered a sackful with ease. Now there were to be sheep here no more. As the ploughman came near to where I was sitting, I watched the skill with which he levered the blades in the turning earth. He was young; the unshaven beard on his face was little more than down; but he drove that plough with the skill of a master. He called the steaming horses, Boxer and Captain, to a standstill, let the ropes fall slack, and waited for me to open the conversation. I like the canniness of the countryman, who seems not to be noticing you but who all the while is quietly summing you up, waiting for you to begin talking before he so much as opens his mouth. Townsmen are apt to mistake this for sullenness, or taciturnity, or even sheer dumbness: in reality it is nothing but a quite natural reticence. This young ploughman waited by his horses in a friendly silence. Pointing to the shining tufts of wool I said, 'So it's good-bye to sheep, eh?' He said wheat was to take their place. 'It looks like being worth while at last, with this 'ere Government grant. At least farmer must think so, or he wouldn't be ploughing all this up, wasting a whole year, too, growing nothing.' I asked him if he was ploughing the whole twenty-two acres alone. 'No,' he replied; 'but tractor broke down this mornin'.' Though he made no comments, I fancied he had his own thoughts on the matter: every true ploughman knows that, whatever the advantages of the tractor, it can never be so thorough, so effective in the long run as the plough. 'Come up, Boxer!' he said and with a smile bade me good-day. I watched the bright blade, gleaming-blue, cleave through the soggy earth. Slowly he passed across the field, under the winter sun. I got down from the gate and walked on.

Surely one of the most attractive features of an English country road is the hedges that line it on either side. Some people criticize them as wasteful, maintaining that they not only take up valuable space but render crops within a full yard of them rank and useless. Nevertheless, I hope the English farmer will never become so skimpy-minded as to do away with them altogether in favour of the more economical fence. When I remember the roses that spray over them in summer, and the berries that brighten them in winter, the birds that build their nests in them, their gay ropes of blackthorn and hawthorn, I am inclined to call it prodigality rather than wastefulness. As I passed along between the hedges yesterday afternoon, it is true I did not see many flowers – a golden flower or two of furze, that persistent bush which the wily young lady in the old rhyme called to her aid, when she said that she would marry her lover as soon as the furze stopped blossoming – but if there were few flowers and almost as few birds, at least there were the hedges themselves to admire. In that particular locality they had all been newly laid down. With a practised eye, some hedger had picked out those boughs that would best serve his purpose, cutting all the rest away near the roots. Then he had chopped at the selected boughs until they could be bent almost flat to the earth, leaving one side of the bark and some of the wood intact, for the sap to flow in. Lastly he had driven in an upright at every certain distance, the height of the desired hedge, slanted the half-chopped boughs all in one direction, bound them to the uprights, and then neatly 'heathered' the hedge along the top.

Leaving the Duntisbournes on my left, as I had been told to do, eventually I came to a signpost pointing to Edgeworth. By now the sun was gone, hidden in a rising fog. The trees stood round me, taller than reality, ghostly, dripping from their branches little drops of water that made a tinkling music as they fell. I climbed and at last came out on to the open wold. A fringe of snow lay under the hedge, left over from a recent fall, waiting, as the countryman likes to suppose, for the next. A roadman who was working up here talked about other snows in other years. The road was high up and caught the wind badly. He could remember how rough it had been in the fall of seven years ago, dating the years, as countrymen do, by some such natural event as a storm, a late hard frost, or a flood. He painted me rough pictures of the drifts in the 'narrows', as he called them, where it had been impossible to pass. Almost regretfully he said that we don't get the snows to-day that we used to. He could recall, as a child, the Cotswold farmers up here bringing out logs and dragging them through the snow themselves to make some sort of a way. 'An' if the sheep got caught out in a bad fall,' he said, 'the only way shepherd could tell where they was, was by the little holes in the snow made by their hot breath. An' if the holes got trodden in, why, of course the sheep was sufficated.'

At Edgeworth, through the thickening fog, I heard the whirr of a threshing-machine. I found the farmyard as busy as only a farmyard can be, when the threshers are in possession. Though it was beginning to get dark, the men still worked on the stacks, forking the wheat into the feeder and trundling the sacks away to the barn. While the engine droned on beside us, the driver pointed out to me that the stack they were threshing just now was already a twelve-month old. 'But that one over there,' he said, wiping his hands on the oily rag, 'is two years old.' It was the same tale as the field of sainfoin that was being converted into wheat. This farmer, like the other, was at last finding it worth while to market his corn. I noticed that all the stacks in the yard were built on 'staddles', those mushroom stones which one finds only in the Cotswolds, and even then more often in gardens, for ornament, than in the farmyards, where they rightly belong. Their purpose is to keep the rats from getting at the wheat, the spreading tops preventing them from climbing up off the ground. I stood for a while watching the pleasant activity about me, but soon it was time to be moving, before the fog became too thick. 'Nigh dark enough,' said the driver, 'to call it a day. . . . Good-night.'

Then the Full Corn in the Ear (1937–1966)

To Essex Again

Each time I return to Essex after any considerable period of absence, I am astonished anew at the vastness and brightness of its skyscape. The horizons are so distant, the sun's arc so wide; one is invigorated by such an excess of light. It was like this when I came back to Essex in May 1937 for the last and best time. There was also another familiar feature – a cold wind that blew in from the North Sea with a sting of winter in its tail. The cowslips were just coming out in the wide grass verges, cold and brittle to pick, and in the hedges where the blackthorn flowers were already disappearing, the first small bunched leaves were unwillingly opening. It was a good time for returning and I was in an exuberant mood. The European situation was worse than ominous but for the moment I determined to ignore it as much as possible and savour to the full the pleasure of being in Essex again – with a craft to my hand, this time, and a moderate but comforting contract in my pocket for two more books. One of these I had nearly finished before leaving Allanhay, the other was presently almost to write itself.

Newport is only a dozen or so miles away from Finchingfield, where I now settled down and Wimbish even less; yet despite having lived in the area I had not visited the village before. I remember it always used to be referred to by my Newport friend as if it were an odd sort of place at the back of beyond. I got the impression that it was even odder than Thaxted and in those days that was saying a good deal. Well, it was my village now and I would see for myself how different it was from other villages and in what way. I soon came to the conclusion that although its degree of oddity was no greater than in other villages, it was certainly unique in character. 'All villages,' H.E. Bates has said, 'are the same. Pretty, idyllic, sequestered, old-fashioned, pastoral – you may call them what you will, but they are all of them sweet-shelled nuts with small bitter kernels.' Perhaps, upon my first return I enjoyed the sweetness somewhat at the expense of the bitterness – that would come soon enough. Something invaluable is gained in first impressions, before criticism pares away any excess – something that will never be repeated; and we do well to let them have their way with us while they may. I have lived in Finchingfield for a score of years now and both place and people have with time become more endearing; but never since that first summer of my arrival have they had the same lyric appeal. I found those immediately pre-war years in Finchingfield as exciting as they were rewarding, not only because once again I was able to indulge that exploration of the new which is manna to any writer but also because, though I scarcely realized it at the time, I was ideally placed to examine and enjoy in detail a village that still retained more than most the character of a day and way of life that was so soon to disappear entirely. There were moments, and I remember them so clearly yet, when I sensed that I had slipped back into another century. John Clare would have been at home in the Finchingfield of these days. Even Bewick would have found much the same kind of subject at hand for his vivid engravings of rural life as he had in the eighteenth century. I lived some way out of the village on rising ground and my first glimpse of it was of a close cluster of thatch and half-timbered cottages surmounted by the square Norman tower of the church and the bold silhouette of the post-type windmill. Wood-smoke rose from the chimneys and put an acrid scent into the chilly evening air. At the forge, Sam the blacksmith, unwilling to go home, leaned over the hatch in conversation with his cronies. A round and jolly lady stood in the middle of the road waving her arms to attract somebody to run an errand for her – this was Olga Stock. And Freddie Dare sauntered in his garden in the dusk, taking a look around, his hands folded behind his back. From outlying farms the men were coming home, some shuffling along with a sack on their backs, their hob-nailed boots striking occasional sparks from the road and some on bicycles which they rode so slowly it was a wonder they did not fall off. And all had a word for Freddie and he for them. His farming days were over and he was enjoying a spare but happy retirement. One picked him out at once in the village, not so much because he asserted himself as because his vitality, even at that age, was so compelling – he attracted one's attention by just being himself, vivid, original and homely-wise. I met him that first evening and at once determined to know much more of him, little imagining that it was he who would put my first Finchingfield book, ready-made, or almost so, into my hands.

A Trayful of Cherries

'I ain't had no education,' said Freddie one day: 'I only speak of my own experience.' Such a claim might suggest the boaster; but all Freddie's life has been an open-handed acceptance of experience, with the result that he has harvested a store of direct knowledge that could not have been won from teachers and books. Many countrymen have this store of direct knowledge, gained from an observation necessarily close and exact; but it is a knowledge that is often very limited in scope and bigoted in application. Freddie has something of an advantage over such countrymen in that he has not only travelled farther than most of them but has been endowed by nature with a vivid, individual mind. If the poet is he who, taking nothing for granted, sees all things afresh through the lens of his own eye, then assuredly there is something of the poet, rough and untutored though it may be, in Freddie. Far as he has travelled, and much as he has seen on the way, he remains at the end of the journey essentially simple, or, as we say, country-minded, wise only in a wisdom that has nothing whatever to do with scholarship. But then, as he himself said on another occasion: 'Scholards are often more dense than the likes o' us, now ain't they?'

School, in so far as Freddie ever attended one, was in fact mainly considered as somewhere to send him out of the way. After all, the times when a child of seven was wanted for work on the farms or in the fields only amounted to a fraction of the year and the jobs to which he could be put were severely restricted: for the rest, therefore, he was just another mouth to be fed, another body to be clothed. And school, anyway, cost money. If there was only one eligible child in a family, the charge was twopence a week; if two, three-halfpence; if three or more, as in the Dare family, a penny. But even a penny was not always easy to come by, and in any case might be better spent on other things. If Freddie's mother, therefore, felt herself able (or inclined) to spare a penny for him on Monday mornings, which were paying-in days, he would hand it up to his teacher upon arrival, see the morning through with what patience he could, and as likely as not never go near the school again all the rest of the week. (Unless, of course, the time was approaching for some village treat to which school attendance would entitle him or from which non-attendance would debar him.) And so, while the other children sat over their lessons – guiding their squealing pencils across the slates and then obliterating their laborious efforts with a smeared spurt of saliva – Freddie wandered with whatever friend he could find in field or wood, and by the river, learning a lore that would never fail him. And he has never regretted such truancies. 'I weren't no good at school, anyway,' he will say, as if in the eyes of any sensible person this must clinch the matter.

If, so far as Freddie could see, there was little reason for attending school, neither was there much reason why he should spend his stolen freedom at home. He would only have been set to do some irksome task. So he went birds'-nesting, or he lay on his stomach on the grassy river-bank, watching for trout, or he learned to snare rabbits in the woods – and incidentally, to keep out of the way of the keepers; and in doing all these things, he acquired a knowledge of nature that might well be the envy of many a trained naturalist. When he did finally venture home again, there was little enough to evoke in him any eager anticipation. Perhaps Mrs Dare would be boiling some dumplings and a scrap of pork for her husband's tea as soon as he came in from the fields. But all Freddie was given before being packed off to bed, out of the way, was a couple of 'floaters'. A pinch of flour, dipped in the water in which the dumplings were boiling, was rolled out between the thumb and the ball of the hand to about the size of a biscuit, fried, and then sprinkled with a spoonful of sugar. 'And it had to do,' said Freddie: 'there weren't no pickin' and choosin', and leavin' bits about, like there is to-day. We had sand for carpet then; and if we ever dropped a mossel of food on the floor, father 'ud say: "Pick it up. A little sand won't hurt you. It'll clear the bowels." 'Yes,' Freddie continued, 'sand was all the carpet we ever had at home. And it was the same in most of the cottages – unless you like to count a sack spread in front of the fire and another by the door to wipe our feet on. Mats ain't no good anyway, when you're allus a-comin' in from the fields with a peck o' clay hangin' on your boots. There was a rummy ol' chap used to ride round the village every Saturd'y, sellin' sand for sprinklin' on the floors. He drove a couple of donkeys, I remember. Each day the sand was gently brushed over, to take the dirty surface off; then a-Saturd'y we'd buy a quart of nice new sand from this 'ere chap with the donkeys; and when we'd cleaned out all the stale stuff, we used to spread it down. Very nice it looked, too: yellow and clean on the bricks.'

'Floaters', it is true, belonged mainly to the lean days; but after all, it was the lean days that predominated in the lives of the farm-labourers of that time. He was therefore a disproportionately jubilant little boy who, sometimes, would be sent down the village to the butcher's shop, jug in hand, to fetch home free blood and a pennyworth (or even two pennyworth) of suet. From this his mother would make black puddings for the family. They were eaten with much relish on the day they were cooked and again, with rather less relish, the day after, when they were cut up and toasted. Meat, as a rule, meant 'pluck' – the heart, liver and lungs of a pig. A 'pluck' cost about tenpence; and, since no scrap of it must be wasted, it was concocted into various dishes and made to eke out the best part of a week. Another dish Freddie recalls from those days was lamb's-tail pudding. 'Many's the time I've et lamb's-tail puddin',' he said, 'and thought nothin' could be nicer. There's a lot of goodness in a lamb's tail. You peel back the skin and break the bone off with your teeth. Very sweet the gristle is: you'd never believe.'

Black puddings and 'pluck' and lamb's-tail puddings, however, were delicacies – tasty feasts in a year-long Lent of mainly bread and potatoes. 'And I can remember somethin' else,' Freddie went on. 'Bloaters were cheaper than they are now, I dunno for why. There was several men used to bring 'em round the village, two for three-ha'pence. Now, my brother Tom was a good few years older'n me, and at the time I'm tellin' you of he used to goo to wukk along o' father. So p'raps one day there'd be a couple of bloaters waitin' for Tom and father when they come home to tea: I could smell mother a-cookin' 'em. Oh, dear, it *did* used to make my mouth water! But they weren't for me. So what do you think I did? When Tom an' father had finished their tea, I used to get hold of them bones and toast 'em in front of the fire. Then I'd break 'em up into little bits and suck all the juice out of 'em. I used to eat the tail, too, and them stiff, prickly ol' fins. But what could you expect, come to think of it, with money as scarce as 'twas?'

And what could you expect from such a hungry, growing boy but that sometimes he should try to compensate himself for such a hard lack by minor thefts? More often than not the thefts would end in a thrashing – or 'lamming', as it is generally called in these parts. Indeed, lammings evidently played quite an important part in Freddie's early life. Not that he minded – or, at least, that is how he views the matter now, from the comfortable perspective of old age. 'I expect we deserved all we got,' he once said to me; 'and if we didn't they didn't do us no harm!'

One spring morning, when the fruit-trees were in bloom, I met Freddie and his cousin Jim on the Green. Out of the clear blue sky a cold east wind was blowing, scattering the white petals in a shower and belying the brilliance of the sunshine. As usual, Freddie wore no overcoat: only his red hands and the watery film over his eager blue eyes suggested that this stocky, straight-backed old man was even aware of the piercing wind. Jim, on the other hand, was muffled up in a long and much-too-tight overcoat somebody had given him, and he kept both hands rammed down as far as possible into its ample pockets. A friendly mouse of a man, Jim is the very opposite to his cousin; a childlike smile plays continually about his crinkled lips and his customary share in the conversation is no more than an occasional, 'That's so, Freddie; that's so!' For one brief spell this morning, however, he managed to monopolize the talk.

Freddie had been angered by some child's flagrant misdeed which he had just witnessed and which had gone unpunished. 'A good hard lammin' was what *he* wanted,' he said. 'He ought to have had my dad for a father; eh, Jim?' 'That's so, Freddie,' responded Jim; 'that's so!' And then, twinkling with unusual playfulness, he continued: 'There wur a whole lot o' lammin's about in our young days. I recollect me an' some more of us was bathin' one day down in the sluice. 'Tweren't no more than a foot or so deep, but we used to splash the water over one another and scurry about there like a lot of dabchicks. Then all of a sudden I see my mother come tearin' hell-for-leather across the Green, after me. She had some steam in her, did ol' Betsy. But I was one too many for her! I runned away in my little skin, for all I was worth, and hid in an ol' tumble-down shed what wur up behind the mill. But of course I had to goo home at last, and there was ol' Betsy a-waitin' for me. A proper lammin' she give me, as soon as ever she got hold of me.'

Meanwhile, Freddie, impatient, as I suspected, that anybody so meek and undramatic as Jim should thus occupy all the attention, busied himself refilling his pipe and seemed not to be listening. But as soon as the pipe was drawing well, and a silence announced that Jim had at last concluded his mumbled interruption, he pointed the clay stem across the Green to where some garden trees were hanging over the river, and said: 'I've just been thinkin' of somethin'. You see that cherry-tree that's in full bloom over there? Well, that's reminded me of another lammin' I had when I was no more'n eight, or perhaps nine, years old. I'll tell you.'

It is part of the intangible reward of a life devoted to the unspectacular routine of a single village, from boyhood to old age, that every tree in it, every nook, every stone almost, should be sufficient to call to mind some forgotten incident. A village, to the native mind, is made up of the lives of those who have lived in it, and their memorials are less in the lichened headstones of the churchyard than in the lanes where they walked and the fields where they worked. And so, as Freddie stared across the Green to the flowering cherry-tree by the river-side, I could see that his mind was spanning the years as easily as the little brick bridge, nearby, spanned the meagre water that flowed underneath.

'In old Mrs Tullen's days,' I heard him saying, 'that were the head cherry-tree in all the village: a proper beauty. You see where the river runs through the garden there? Well, at that time it was a Mrs Tullen as lived there – a nice ol' lady she was, too – and I remember she allus wore a Pompadour dress: never saw her in anything else. One day, some of us kids waded through the water till we got so's we could pull the cherries off the tree. Mind you, it weren't deep enough to drown a stickleback in; and there we stood, pullin' down as many cherries as ever we could lay hands on. We didn't know as all the time Mrs Tullen was a-watchin' us from her back winders.

'When we'd all cleared off, she sent somebody up home to say if we didn't goo down an' apologize, she'd have us all locked up. So we put our heads together.' Here Freddie's laughing eyes entirely belied the gravity with which he tried to inform his words. 'We put our heads together,' he continued, 'and decided we'd better goo an' say we were sorry. I can see us all a-troopin' down the hill now, meek as butter. We knocked at the door and stood there, with our caps in our hands, wondering whatever she would say. But all she said was, "Wait a minute," and then disappeared down the passage. When she came back, she was carryin' a trayful of fine ripe cherries. "There you are," she said, "take 'em over there on the grass and eat 'em." You could a-knocked me down with a feather. That's where we sat, just over there on the corner of the Green. And when we took the empty tray back again, she gave us each a penny. "Now you see," she said, "if only you'd asked me, you could have had as many cherries as you wanted."

'Of course, we stopped at the shop on our way home and bought some sweets o' some sort. But father got wind of what had happened and give me a lammin' for not takin' the penny home. Leastways, he tried to; but I dodged round the table, with my eye on the door at the bottom of the stairs, and I'd lifted that latch an' bolted up to the bedroom afore he could get at me. I was spry enough when I was young, I can tell you!'

'Aye, that's so,' said Jim, shaking his smiling, wasted face; 'that's so, Freddie.'

Then there was that trivial but none the less memorable occasion when, at about the age of twelve, Freddie and one of his young friends indulged in an uncomfortable orgy of sausages. One morning, as he was getting ready to go to work, his father discovered that he had no tobacco. The village shop not being yet open, he left instructions for Freddie to bring some tobacco out to Titley Farm, where he was working, later in the morning. 'On the way there,' said Freddie, 'I met young Tom Bradley and asked him to come along o' me. So he did. I ought to a-told you that the farmer out at Titley them days was a great big man, weighed twenty-two stone or so, and very fond of sausages. The farm was reg'lar well known for its sausages. I dessay they'd fry more'n a couple of pounds at a time, and there'd be Farmer Bentham pullin' 'em out of the fryin'-pan while they was still fryin'. Well, when young Tom Bradley an' me got to Titley, and had given father his tobacco, the gal there said she'd a skuttle wanted mendin' and would we take it back along with us to the smith's in the village?

She gave us some sausages for our trouble. So off we went, and when we'd got as far as Barn Meadow, Bradley said, "Let's 'ave some of them sausages!" We hadn't no bread or nothin', but that didn't matter to us. We polished off a tidy few and then we went on a bit farther. I expect we were a long time on the way: you know what boys are! Anyway, time we got as far's Gavin's, young Bradley said he felt peckish again, and why didn't we finish the sausages up altogether? I took the skuttle to the smith's and then went home.

'"Come on," says mother, "here's your dinner." But I didn't want no dinner, did I? I only wanted to goo off and play again. "Ain't you well, or somethin'?" she says. "I'm all right," I says; "but I don't want no dinner." "Then you've been up to somethin'," she says; "I'm sure you have." That evenin', when father came home from wukk, he said, "What about havin' some of them sausages for tea, mother?" She asked him whatever sausages he meant. "Why, them young Freddie brought back from Titley this mornin', of course," he said. And there was I, sittin' in my chair and supposin' everything was all right. I felt terrible: my hands fell down to my sides like wet sacks. "Then what d'you do with 'em?" father said. "Et 'em," I said; and with that he fetched me a clout beside the head. Still, I'd enjoyed them sausages; and one lammin' more or less didn't make much difference, did it? Only it didn't seem hardly fair young Tom Bradley shouldn't have a lammin' too, I remember!'

Other thrashings Freddie has told me of, at one time and another, but one must suffice here, and that I only relate because it offers a preliminary glimpse of the casualness with which minor (and sometimes major) illnesses were treated by the poorer villagers sixty or seventy years ago. Whether it was poverty, or lack of belief in the efficacy of doctors, or somewhat of both, that prompted such casualness I do not know; but certainly there was none of the precaution and carefulness which we are all invited to indulge in to-day. Freddie had the usual attack of measles. His mother left the cottage in the morning to go out to work in the fields and told him he must stop indoors while she was away. 'But,' said Freddie, 'it was summer-time, and how *could* I stop indoors? Of course I couldn't; so, time she was out in the fields somewheres, I slipped off down to the river and bathed – spots an' all. "Didn't I tell you you was to stop indoors?" mother said, when she found out where I'd been; and you can bet she gave me a good strapping. All the same, them measles disappeared. Why, I can remember two brothers who took the scarlet fever and nobody knew they'd had it till they were better: *they* never went to no 'orspital. It was some old woman in the village that cured 'em – I dunno how. And the cottage wasn't disinfected afterwards, nor nothin' like that.

'No,' Freddie continued, 'we never went to the doctor's for anything but toothache and broken bones, though there were two of 'em in the village. Mostly we used to buy a lotion and little penny boxes of ointment from an old witch of a woman who lived here. The lotion was made out of shirt-button seeds' (mallow, whose seeds somewhat resemble shirt buttons) 'and young elder shoots; and the ointment was made from sheep's droppings and lard. That ointment 'ld fetch the poison out of anything. There's a power of healin' in manure, do you know that? Take a horse now, what's got the thrush: there ain't nothin' that'll do him as much good as some dung rammed into his hoof. Manure – and herbs: there's a wonderful lot of curin' power in both. I dessay if we knew all the things the herbs of the fields was good for, we wouldn't need no doctors at all. But nowadays it's all chemicals: you're stuffed with chemicals till you're purty nigh *made* of 'em.'

Freddie's talk is often fruitful of informative minutiae – details which, as even the most academic historians are beginning to realize, are sometimes quite as illuminative of the story of man's evolution as the more resounding developments. In fact it is in the conversation of just such vivid old men as Freddie that we of a later generation may best sense the significance of the change that has come over the English countryside during the past three-quarters of a century. A severe drought, for instance, had reduced the outlying parts of Finchingfield to a total dependence upon the village water-cart. It is a sadly familiar happening in parts of East Anglia. The local water-supply (mainly a matter of ponds and surface-wells) gives out somewhere about the middle of August. For a week or two nothing whatever is done by the authorities, and the cottagers are compelled to wash their clothes (and their children) in the green slime of some cattle-pond, and to drink what the men (after a heavy day's work on the farm) can bring home from a nightly rummage round the fields. Then at last some slow-moving contractor gets the order and water is brought out from the village, in uncovered tanks, to the extravagant extent of a couple of pails to every house. This state of affairs probably continues until the beginning of December. I know this will sound to some an unfair distortion of the truth: as a matter of fact, it is even less than the truth of what happened in the outlying parts of Finchingfield during the summers of 1937 and 1938. Such, then, was the subject of a conversation I was having with Freddie one day, our talk revolving round the fact that, although to-day electric light can be found in the most out-of-the-way places, an adequate water-supply for everybody is still a Utopian dream. Freddie deplored the lack of water as much as I did, but he was not at all convinced that electric light was an unadulterated blessing.

'We used rush candles at home when I was a boy,' he said. 'They cost a penny a time and were made out of the peeled pith of rushes dipped into melted taller. Sometimes we even used to make our own. I'd be sent out to get some of the biggest and best rushes down in the water-meadows; and then all the peel was taken off, except for a couple of ribs runnin' from top to bottom. You know, to hold the pith together. To my way o' thinkin', they gave a poor sort of light: when you'd lit one, you wanted to light another to see it by. But there, we didn't read and we mostly went to bed early, so what did it matter? Besides, flitterin' little things as they was, they didn't injure the eyesight like all this glarin' light we get nowadays. Too much brilliance an' too much readin', that's what ruins the eyes.

'There was only one newspaper used to come into our house. It went the round from family to family – a ha'penny sheet that came out once a week. So you see we didn't have papers lyin' all over the house like you see everywhere to-day. Fire had to be lighted with wisps of straw. . . . Nor there weren't no letters, either – not to speak of. You could have put all the mail that came into the parish in your overcoat pocket. If we 'ad one letter in our family in four years, I reckon that was about all. But then you see there wasn't more than one in every three or four cottages that could read; so when anybody did get a letter, it had to be took from neighbour to neighbour, till it was all spelled out proper; and you can bet there weren't much secret about the news time it was all pieced together! The postman – we called 'im the letters-man – only used to deliver letters in the village; and folk that lived upland, same as you do, had to goo and fetch their mail. Or p'raps the man that kept the post office would ask somebody if they happened to be gooin' that way. "Are you gooin' up past Yeldham's?" he'd say; "because if you should see Ben Notley you might tell 'im there's a letter waitin' here for him."'

Thereupon Freddie went on to tell me a tale that is probably apocryphal, a concession, as it were, to his undeniable predilection for the dramatic. It would have been a slight to the artist in him to check this tale, as I think my readers will agree. I have sometimes thought that, with his keen memory, his regard for the potent detail, and his native ability in the manipulation of all the tricks of narrative, Freddie would have made a first-class journalist if the chances had come his way. As it is, his talent for drama has had to content itself with expression in the spoken word. In any company, it is immediately noticeable how he shines out above his fellows. Whoever may be holding the floor when the conversation begins, it will not be long before Freddie, effortlessly and without the slightest suggestion of vanity, takes his place. While others are fumbling for words, their thoughts withheld for lack of the power to express them, he will jump into the arena with a single sentence, pertinent, pungent, and exact. Yet he is a good listener, too: the only trouble being that there are so few among his everyday companions who have as good things to tell as he already knows. He is, in consequence, sometimes called 'an old know-all.' But, as I once heard him say in defence of such an accusation: 'If you *do* know, you do, don't you?' And usually Freddie does know. On this particular occasion, however, I think he was (as I have already suggested) more intent upon providing entertainment than upon supplying exact information. Anyway, here is the tale.

'The post,' he said, 'was brought out from Braintree by cart in them days; and at the time I'm tellin' you of, the job was contracted out to a man that lived over at Benfield. He drove a little closed-in box of a cart, on high wheels, with painted spokes nigh as thin as matches. A mule drew the cart and sometimes you'd meet it fair flyin' along the roads. On the way back to Braintree each night, the postman – he wore a little ol' pill-box hat, I remember – used to call at Finchingfield, Shepfield, and Stalling to pick up the mail-bags. There he sat, perched up on top of his little red cart, in a sort of fenced-in seat. The mail-box was padlocked at the back; and each post-master – or whatever you like to call 'em, for mostly they did a dozen other jobs besides – had his own key. He'd hurry out with the mail-bag, unlock the box, fling the bag in, and then lock it up again. "Night, Joe!" he'd say; and without so much as a word from the driver, or a flick o' the whip, away that ol' mule 'ld goo like a streak of lightnin'. He knew the roads just as well as Joe himself did.

'Well, we used to have rare hard winter weather then – sometimes it 'ld be below zero. More'n once I've played games on the pond when I was a kid: bowlin' for oranges instead of coconuts, you know. Why, the water would be frozen so thick that even the ground underneath was frozen too. But as I was sayin', there'd be ol' Joe, sittin' up there on his high seat, all muffled up to the ears so's you couldn't tell whether he answered you or not. And one mighty cold night, he came rattlin' along the road same as usual, and called at all the post offices like he did every blessed night of the year. It was so cold that whenever he stopped, the post-master just flung the mail-bag into the back of the cart, locked up the box as quick as ever he could, and scuttled off indoors again out of the weather. "Night, Joe!" he called, and away went the mule. When they got to Braintree, they pulled into the post office yard, and somebody came out to collect the bags. "You've had a cold ride to-night, Joe, and no mistake," he said. But Joe never answered a word. He just sat up there on his perch, without so much as movin' a hand – for he was frozen dead in his seat. And nobody ever knowed whereabouts on the road it happened.'

England

There are those who say we should all be glad to be living in this hour. The world is being shaped anew and it is a privilege to be alive while such high things are happening. Well may this be so; yet at this moment I think rather of those who have died already since the outbreak of war, shot down like birds or frozen to death in arctic snows, or cast upon the cold waters to die of exposure or plunged alive to the bottom of the sea, and I wonder what lasting good can come of such violence, such wanton refusal of the life so mysteriously given to us.

I look around me in this quiet village of Finchingfield and all I see to-day speaks of life and hope – the spearing wheat in the fields, the audacious snowdrop buds in the gardens, the rising sap in the frail wands of the willow and the dog-wood, the mating birds and the busy farmers.

Only one thing seems in accord with the destruction that is silently piling up the other side of the North Sea.

Twice or thrice a day the timber-lorries splash down the road past my house, bearing the shorn trunks of oak and elm. They are felling trees on Arley Hall estate. Not one tree here and another tree there, but scores of them, massive trees that have breasted the winds of a century and more, bestowing health and beauty with their green turbulence of leaves.

Ever since the timber valuer arrived, weeks ago, these trees have borne on their trunks the earmark of destruction: like those crosses chalked on the doors of the houses of the Plague, they have proclaimed the pity of their approaching end. And now the end has come. First, their stout bases were hacked away, leaving a litter of bright chips scattered on the ground. Then the tree-fellers arrived, with rope and pulley and crane, and one day the mighty tree shivered and cracked and fell, with bleeding branch and twig.

Surely it should be decreed by law, in any civilized country, that for every tree which is felled another should be planted in its place? It is not enough that the Government should make belated amends by setting up trim forests of spruce, regardless of their suitability to the locality, and each planted in a dead straight line with all its neighbours. The glory of our trees (apart from their usefulness) is in their multitudinous dissimilarity, though indigenous to the district in which they grow. And every man whom chance, or ability, has made the owner of wooded acres should, if compelled to fell, have as much regard for the ultimate renewal of the beauty he has destroyed as he has for the cash with which such destruction has rewarded him. Felling trees to pay off debts which cannot otherwise be met is only robbing Peter to pay Paul; and no property can be said to be well-managed where the best of the timber has been felled to pay off debts, unless that timber is at least replaced with suitable and equivalent young trees.

One of the heartening things about the slaughter of trees on the Arley Hall estate is the almost general reaction of the villagers. Time and again, as the timber-wagons sway and rumble past, I have heard expressions of genuine regret that such denudation is necessary. These trees, we all feel, belong to every one of us and we are the poorer for their disappearance. Not even the fact that we shall be able to share in the spoil really consoles us. There will be 'tops' at one and sixpence a time – enough wood to keep our fires burning through another winter, whatever hardships war may still bring; and even those of us who cannot afford so small an outlay will have chips by the bushel. But the trees will be gone. A loaf of bread is not always better than a poem, even to a starving man.

So the trees go past, bound for the railway station and thence for the timber-yard. Next to go, we hear, will be the spruce woods – 'just the right size for pit-props.' Once again the war is denuding the countryside, as it did a quarter of a century ago, of the trees that helped to give us health and sustain our spirits. There are war's scars on the body of the countryside – scars it will take years to heal, if ever.

Otherwise, there is still little enough in Finchingfield to suggest approaching holocaust. More lads have gone into the Army to learn to endure their firm young flesh stretched upon the rack of war, and a few older men are volunteering while there is still time for them at least to choose in which of the Services they shall offer to die. Black-outs have all but hardened into a habit and, although we no longer carry our gas-masks, they lie ready to hand for the return of the day when we must. Squadrons of bombers have come back into our skies, but instead of rushing to the window to look at them we merely register the boom of their flight in the pauses of our conversation. Is it a lessening of fear or a gradual acceptance of fatalism? Or merely the sheer impossibility, here in the quiet, awakening countryside, of imagining the full horror of what may befall?

'I ain't goin' to wear no gas-masks,' says Ann Bright; 'no, that I ain't. There's a little ol' cupboard at the top of our stairs, and I shall hide in there till it's all over. And I 'ont come out for nobody.'

Meanwhile, these green spears of life, these fattening buds on the trees – all the frail portents of the resurgence of spring – have an added poignancy this year, an added appeal to our sensibilities. Hod is busy with his lambing and the sight of him slouching through the mud, with a lamb under each arm, its long legs dangling awkwardly against his hips, is somehow sharpened in the mind by contrast with the dark thoughts against which it is set. He is leading his sheep into the fold for the night; dams, heavy with their undropped lambs, and day-old lambs that totter over the furrows on legs that have not yet found their native cunning. The baa of the anxious mothers and the answering bleat of the straying young is as much part of the music of spring as the tentative stanzas of that speckled cock-thrush perched against the sky, and both seem more precious now than ever before.

But most precious of all perhaps is the sight of Jim Adams ploughing in Humpback Field. I expect it is only my fancy but birds always seem to be more than usually plentiful in the fields where Jim is ploughing, as if they knew he liked their company and would do them no harm.

At any rate, all day he has been moving slowly across the field surrounded by a veritable cloud of seagulls blown in from the coast as if, all that distance away, the rumour had somehow reached them that Jim was at plough. There must be well over a hundred. They wheel and cry low over the field till Jim has crested the rise, and then they glide down to the newly turned furrows and settle in thick clots of snowy white. Jim turns at the headland, advancing down the field again; and as the plough draws near they rise, some seeming to wait until the horses' hooves must trample them, and circle overhead, closing Jim in a flurry of gleaming wings.

Here and there among the flashing white horde are a crow or two, croaking mourners at a wedding feast.

'Them gulls are so tame,' says Jim, 'they just stand there as if it was *you* who'd got to get out of the way! But I recollect a chap once, when he was out ploughing somewhere, chucked a spanner or something at one and killed it – a seagull it was. Well, he never had no gulls following him after that. They stayed over the hedge in the next field and waited till he was out of the way.'

Leaving Jim under his cloud of white wings I walk home towards the village.

There are moods of the spirit when the bright, particular things of everyday – houses, gates, the way a tree leans, the motion of a man at work in the fields – seem suddenly of more than ordinary beauty. They are like poems before the poet has spoiled them in the endeavour to chain them with the discipline of words.

I pass a villager pushing a tumbledown pram in which a child sits heaped over with kindling. The setting sun shines in the woman's eyes and something of the madonna shows through the weary lines of her peasant face. 'Good-night,' she says; 'good-night,' and the goodwill that prompts her words is part of the basis of that common understanding (would we but give it play) between person and person, village and village, nation and nation.

I pass lonely farm cottages set back from the road, to whose hearths the men will soon be returning across the evening fields. And they are fixed in my mind as the very type of all men's desire for the fulfilment of his 'potentiality to love and to be loved'. The faggots leaning against the chimney-stack, the grindstone under the apple-tree in the garden, the few chickens in their run, and the plot of garden waiting to be sown – I see it all as a promise of immense possibilities. Even the brick bungalows, and the staring red council cottages, seem suddenly endearing: homes, loved hearths, centres of that creative love which is the root of all our endeavour, however brief and small.

And as I loiter here and there, talking with first one and then another, I forget for the moment the misery that shadows all our lives in this first faint prelude of spring; I am only aware of the simple happiness that comes of innocent communion, man with man.

In all the shires of England, I think, such cottages wait in the fields and by the roadside, gilded with the setting sun that brings the men home from their work. This is England, though ninety per cent of her population dwells in the towns; for here the first condition of life is not gain but service – service of the land that feeds us and gathers us at last into its fecund darkness. Here men work creatively, ploughing, sowing, harvesting. Here, if anywhere, that goodwill may thrive, which, in spite of wars, shall at last bind the ends of the earth in the bonds of true fellowship.

Mutz

It is as if the whole round earth beneath our feet had gone dead: as if we were living now on another moon.

I look out of the window into the garden (or where the garden ought to be) and I see none of those comforting rings of bare earth in the snow, as if the plants' warm breath had melted a clearing round their living leaves. The wallflowers and Brompton stocks, which I planted in the autumn, stand out of the snow like grey rags tied to a stick; there is no warm breath in *those* leaves to melt away the snow. And that apple-tree, round whose base there should by now be showing the golden bulbs of the aconite – can such a filigree of iron ever break into a million down-flushed buds? As for the vegetable garden, the spade has not yet been invented which could dig up my leeks or parsnips, frozen into the earth like fossils in a rock. The whole universe has lost its breath; and in this arctic moment it seems to be touch and go whether it will ever find it again.

Mutz died last night, and the only way of burying him this morning was by thawing the ground a little with a bonfire. His death was itself something of a symbol – for me, at least – of the withering cold that has had us all in its grip these last few days. Eight months old, he was still not much more than midway between kitten and cat: a frolicking, irresponsible little creature one minute and already a not quite staid tom the next.

There had seemed nothing whatever wrong with him, no possible reason why he should die. And then yesterday afternoon he suddenly sickened. I made him a warm bed by the fire, and, since he refused all food and drink, left him to sleep. Sleep, I know, will cure most of the ills that cat-flesh is heir to, and so I did not worry. But the sickness increased. Nothing I could do seemed to relieve him; as soon as the bout was over, he would curl up in his rags again, look at me appealingly, and then bury his shivering head.

Once he dragged himself out of his bed, crawled across the floor on sagging legs, and made his way to the saucer in the kitchen where he always has his milk. When he failed to return, I went out to see what had happened, and there he lay in front of his saucer, his mouth inside it, and all the milk spilt over the floor. I warmed and diluted a little; but however much he may have desired it, he was unable to lap it up; and so I carried him back to his bed beside the fire.

I asked where I could for advice, but nobody knew what to suggest. Country cats are expected to look after themselves. 'Let him sleep it off,' was the general answer to my query; but as the evening advanced, and Mutz continued to lie there, questioning me every now and then, as I imagined, with his dulled eyes ('*Isn't* there anything you can do?'), I found it increasingly difficult to believe that sleep alone would mend all in the end.

To spend one's grief on a dying cat is usually considered a sentimental indulgence, and I admit I have seen instances all too many of people whose grief for suffering animals is only matched by their lack of grief for suffering mankind. 'Animals have no souls,' says one friend, a Catholic; 'and so you do wrong to feel too strongly about the death of a cat.' But I find myself preferring the words of another friend: 'The virtue of non-attachment is demonstrated daily,' he says, 'but when creatures of living beauty attach themselves to one, one is willing to sin and take the consequences.'

Certainly Mutz was no great beauty. He belonged to that vast, harum-scarum race of country cats whose family tree is as rank as an elder and quite as ineradicable. But equally certainly he knew how to attach himself to one. All the wiles of the cat tribe who, of all living creatures, best know the art of retaining their independence while at the same time flattering the human desire for a show of complete submission, were his *in excelsis*. He gave, only in so far as it pleased him to give; and in return he got – all he wanted! It was impossible (at least in this household) to deny him. From the moment he crossed the threshold, deep in the safety of a jacket pocket, he ruled the place.

Clearly enough, I recall the occasion when we first brought Mutz home. I had asked the baker to try to find me a cat, knowing his own affection for all cats; and apparently all the mongrels of the parish were passed under review before Mutz was discovered and duly pronounced by him as just the cat for me.

It was Heinz's birthday – his first in England after being hounded out of a Nazified Vienna. With all the Austrian's love of animals and birds (did they not once charter an aeroplane to rescue the blizzard-caught swallows, stranded in the Alps, and carry them into the sunshine of the south?) he had asked me to get a kitten. At first I hesitated, remembering Sam's depredations among the birds in my garden. With the skill of a tight-rope walker, Sam would tread the top of the hedge and pick the naked wretches out of their nests. A family of yellow-hammers, flashing the gold nuggets of their heads in the sun of my garden, is as precious to me as rare flowers are in other gardens, and I did not relish the thought of a second Sam nullifying my pleasure. And there was another thing. Sam was a wanderer and had finally paid the price of his freedom by getting himself caught in a rabbit-snare, an end I was not anxious to have repeated.

But cats are not to be denied by mere humane considerations like these. Their persistence is almost psychic: they get themselves a home in spite of the stoutest denials. If there is somebody in the room who hates cats, it is just her lap and none other they will choose, and the unhappy recipient of their attentions has no alternative but to pretend she feels herself honoured. So with Mutz: in spite of all my determination, he arrived – as if the very stars in their courses had ordained it so.

One evening in July, therefore, we walked over to Nat Swift's to fetch him. The way home took us past Charlie Beslyn's cottage. From behind the leafy screen of his garden he must have been watching us; for that night a Woolworth envelope was handed in at my door, addressed in Charlie's clear, untutored hand. Inside were the following verses:

> The primrose path of happiness
> > Is walked in greatest measure
> By those who seek, and find content
> > In simple childlike pleasures.
> This night I saw two men who found
> > Delight, in simple treasure

By playing with a tiny pet
  To occupy their leisure.
Said Bertha who was with me then
  (I thought I'd better mention)
Just look at those two men out there
  And see how great attention
They're giving to that tiny thing
  A little ball of fluff
A kitten small and black and round
  And yet just big enough
To give them greater happiness
  Than tons and tons of pelf
Or all the pleasures gained by those
  Who pander to theirselves.

To set Charlie's verses down in a book, like this, in all the cool precision of print, is rather like setting a simple, stay-at-home girl in the glare of stage limelight: the original merit eludes the daze of publicity. I include them nevertheless, for they became part of our pleasure in Mutz henceforth.

Not many kittens have a poem sung over their christening. It is true that Mutz never showed any signs of wanting to live up to the dignity thus thrust upon him: to the end he remained plebeian, one of the masses, a cat whose manners were no better than they should have been, and whose name (bestowed impromptu, when his sex rendered irrelevant the original Mitsi) was the only unusual thing about him.

And now he is dead. Rightly or wrongly, proportionately or disproportionately, his dying affected me considerably. I believe now that the significance of the event was somehow rendered the more emphatic by (I know it sounds ridiculous) the weather. I found it impossible to get warm that night. Even when I sat inside the fireplace, logs and coals conspiring together for my comfort, I found the heat more an illusion than a reality. Somewhere inside me a core of cold persisted. And perhaps because of this, the sight of Mutz, incommunicable in his suffering, shivering his life away in that bundle of rags, bit itself the more keenly into my consciousness.

I tried to read, but the picture of a dying cat imposed itself between me and the words. At midnight, unable to do anything more to relieve him, I piled up the fire, tucked Mutz into his rags, and went upstairs to bed. I tried to sleep, but the thought of a dying cat came between me and the oblivion I sought. Finally, at about two-thirty, weary of the attempt to shut him out of my mind, I came downstairs again.

Never, in England, have I known such intentful cold. It seemed to squeeze the breath out of my body, as if I were being clamped in a relentless vice. Now, I felt, was the very zero hour of all this bitter spell of bad weather. In the fireplace was nothing but a heap of ashes. Mutz had crawled out of his bed and lay on the hearthrug a foot or so away. His eyes were open, but there was no meaning left in them. I lifted his paw. It was still warm, but it fell aimlessly out of my fingers.

I covered him over and went back to bed. And as I lay there, shivering, the fact of his death began to assume almost morbid proportions, until it seemed to focus the evil intensity of the cold. The force I had seen at work in the lane outside, piling up those malignant and yet lovely drifts of snow, so silently and so remorselessly, became for the moment identified for me with the death of my cat.

Uneasily at last I slept; and when I came down this morning, Mutz's body was frozen fast to the mat.

Rural Wit

Some villages win a reputation merely by being pretty. The claim has been made for my own village, for instance, that it is 'one of the five prettiest villages in England'; but who awarded the honour, or precisely upon what grounds, I could not discover. Others achieve a reputation by having been the residence of some great man. It matters not how little they thought of him while he was alive; dead, he brings them fame. Selborne *is* Gilbert White, just as Grasmere *is* Wordsworth. But not many villages win a reputation for the abundance of their foolishness – like Yubberton (Ebrington) in the Cotswolds.

In fact I think I might have been inclined to discredit Yubberton if I had not known of a similar instance nearer home. What Yubberton is to the Cotswolds, Coggeshall (if this little country town will excuse comparison with a village) is to Essex; and both have had their peculiar reputation for a long time. John Ray, who collected proverbs as well as plants, and who lived not many miles from Coggeshall, quotes a rural rhyme about the district:

'Braintree for the pure, and Bocking for the poor;
Cogshall for the jeering town, and Kelvedon for the boor.'

I don't know about the others, but Coggeshall is still a place to point the jeering finger at; all in the best of fun, of course. 'That's a rare bit of Coggeshall,' people will say for miles around, when they see something being done in a foolish manner. 'He's a Coxall,' they will say, too, of anybody who invariably behaves in such a way. Indeed, a 'Coggeshall job' is the local expression for any bit of work that is awkwardly done.

Only the other day I heard an example in a second-hand book-shop as far away as the West Country. As soon as I had given the proprietor my address, he said: 'Isn't that near Coggeshall? You know, the place where they chained up a wheelbarrow in a shed, so that it shouldn't go mad after having been bitten by a dog?' I said it was and offered him another tale for his collection about the Coggeshall men who, when they saw the grass growing on their church tower, hoisted up a cow to graze it. But he knew that one, too.

I confess that this good-humoured jeering seems to me rather strange, when one considers the kind of place Coggeshall was and still (in a measure) is. In the fifteenth century it stood second only to such places as Colchester and Norwich for its wool-trade; and in the next century, when the Flemings and Walloons introduced the famous 'bays and says', it could boast an even greater fame. Its specialities included a bay called the 'Coxall minikin' and 'Coggeshall Whites' – 'the best whites in Englande', said John Norden. Paycockes House, close against the main road, still stands to attest both to the wealth and to the good taste of its chief wool-merchant.

Then again, the fine work of the Coggeshall wood-carvers may be seen in many an Essex church, while, as every collector knows, Coggeshall clocks were much esteemed. Tambour lace was made there, and to-day the place has a wide reputation for its seeds.

Why, then, should it have been singled out for 'the jeering town'? Some would probably answer that this was yet another instance of rural wit and humour from the days when countrymen had to provide their own fun or go without. That this is so of Yubberton and other out-of-the-way places, I can well understand. In the Rodings, for instance, it is said that they empty their ponds with a sieve. Well, anything might happen in the Rodings – those lonely parishes, all corn and willows, west of Chelmsford. But Coggeshall? Why should Coggeshall, with its reputable industries and its one-time prosperity, have been made the subject for such ribaldry?

Perhaps the answer lies in this very prosperity. Perhaps a local feeling of envy was responsible.

And so, it may be, some rural wag spread the tale abroad that Coggeshall men put hurdles in the river to turn back the water. He said that when they volunteered to defend their town against Napoleon they were so uncertain of their left and right that the sergeant had to tie a wisp of straw on every right leg and a wisp of hay on every left before he could drill them effectively 'Hay, straw; hay, straw'! It was these same Coggeshall men, too, who, when smallpox was raging over at Colchester, chained up their barrows and coaches so that they shouldn't catch the disease. And again, when they saw that the two windmills outside the town were idle, they pulled one down, because obviously there wasn't enough wind for both.

It was this same wag, perhaps, who put it about that Coggeshall men forgot to put any windows in their church when they built it. They therefore took some hampers and opened them to catch the sunlight, and then, quickly shutting them, wheeled them in barrows into the church and there opened them again to let the light out. And one day, he declared, when the Town Band was practising in an upper room in Stoneham Street, somebody came up and told them how beautiful it sounded down in the street, whereupon, to a man, they left their instruments and went outside to listen.

Of course, this kind of rustic nonsense has its counterpart all over the country, from Darlaston in Staffordshire, where they tried to entice the cock off the church tower weather-vane with split peas, to Towednack in Cornwall, where, in order that they might have summer all the year, they built a wall round the cuckoo. Somewhere in Cumberland, I believe, they are said to have followed the coach in order that they might see the big wheel catch the little one. And isn't it Pershore where they say the cuckoo buys a horse at the local Fair (26 June) and rides away on it?

A jobbing carpenter I know is always trotting out examples of this kind of nonsense. 'Ever heard tell of the man whose ladder wasn't long enough?' he will ask, with a twinkle. 'He sawed a few rungs off the bottom and tied 'em to the top.' Bewick, too, true countryman that he was, made one of his famous tail-pieces out of a similiar instance. A man is shown sawing a bough from a tree and sitting on the wrong end of it to do so. And George Sturt said of the men of Pirbright (a sort of Coggeshall of the South), that they were obliged to look in the puddles before they knew if it was raining. Moreover, these same Pirbrighters drove the fish in the canal under the bridge lest they should get wet.

Well, I suppose one kind of fame is as good as another, in the end; but I wish I knew just why Coggeshall should have achieved this particular kind.

One of the favourite sayings of my father, who was a countryman born and bred, was 'It doesn't take *us* long to do a five minutes' job!' And if anybody was out and about unusually early in the morning, he would say to them: 'You must have got up before you went anywhere!' To the townsman, I dare say, there would not seem to be anything very funny in either of these quips, but the dyed-in-the-wool countryman would respond at once with a chuckle. I am not going to defend country humour, much less to try and define it; all I want to insist upon is that anybody with a gill of country blood in his veins would recognize my father's sayings as good examples.

It is one of the most attractive features of country humour that it never quite loses its freshness. It may be passed on from generation to generation, but it remains a coin whose mintage is never dulled with use. The same may be said of other country expressions which are not necessarily humorous at all – metaphors and likenesses and odd phrases which, once coined, have never gone out of currency. 'You might just as well follow the hare with a tabor' is a saying that has an old-time ring about it, as if it dated back to the morris-dancing England of long ago. Very likely it does; but it was only last year I heard it used, in Gloucestershire, during the course of an ordinary country conversation. And for how long have the cottagers here in my own village been saying, in moments of elation, that they feel 'as happy as all the birds'?

The fact is, of course, that poetry comes naturally to the countryman. (Or should I say, alas, it used to come naturally?) His senses have not been dulled, as the townsman's too often have been, and the result is that he is inevitably graphic in his speech. 'Her's nothin' but an owd yowe dressed up lamb fashion', is the description I remember hearing, also in Gloucestershire, of a togged-up woman who was old enough to have known better: 'I wouldn't be seen with her in a field of tinkers!'

The countryman's concern is first and foremost with things. It is in the nature of his job, all the day and all the year, that this should be so. Accordingly, his speech always tends to be factual. Of an animal in prime condition he will say: 'It was as good a beast as ever got into a skin.' Expressing his scorn of a fat, lazy woman, a Gloucestershire farmer once said to me: 'Don't thee ever wed such a great mullock of a creature, they uses up all their energy to carry their carcasses about.' And it was a Yorkshire farmer whom I heard say to a novice who was helping to stack the corn: 'Put thee's backside round t'other way, lad!'

In conversation with one of my neighbours the other day, she said: 'That puts me in mind of old Susan. She had only one tooth in her head. She used to fold the table-cloth on it, I remember.' Try and describe Susan's action for yourself. Can you do it in as few words as my neighbour, who never went to school? Or as graphically, however many words you use? You and I, in losing something of this over-riding interest in things, have lost, too, the vivid speech that goes with it. How we should have to fumble for words to express, for instance, the action of manure on the land. But the Essex countryman, born in arable and bred in the art of mucking it, says, quite simply, 'That'll *mend* it!'

Gradually, of course, country speech is tending to become as dull and ordinary as town speech, just as country humour is tending to lose its characteristic flavour – as characteristic as the flavour of a hazelnut, or a wild strawberry. That old Gloucestershire farmer, whom I have already mentioned, was telling me how, when he was young, many of the farm-hands in his village would only have their hair cut once a year – the Saturday before the local Fair. There was, he said, a certain carter, William, whose hair was very long indeed. Working under him was a boy who, in the enthusiasm of his first grown-up job, irritated William by his unduly frequent instructions to the horses. 'Het!' and 'Wo!' he would say, again and again, until William could bear it no longer. 'Shut thee's rattle, boy!' he said. Much hurt in his pride, the boy pondered his revenge, and presently this is what he came out with. 'Willum, when be'st thee goin' to have thy yare cut? 'Cause I'll bespake the fleece for maaster's staddle!' Would the country boy's humour of to-day rise to that?

Nevertheless, there still are plenty of villages, up and down the land, where the men and women use the good old words (though they may drive a tractor instead of a team of horses and listen to the radio every night) and where true rural wit and humour still survive.

In one such village, and it is less than fifty miles from the heart of London itself, a certain labourer is a standing joke even to-day because it took him so long to make up his mind to get married. Sunday after Sunday, for I don't know how many years, he cycled to the nearby hamlet where his lady-love lived. His week's washing was always tied in a bundle on the carrier. 'There goes old Wally a-courtin',' was the regular comment; but there was never any rumour of an approaching marriage. At last, however, he did somehow manage to bring it off. 'But not avore he'd wore out three door-scrapers,' the village said. And long after he is dead I am sure he will still be known as 'old Wally – who wore out three door-scrapers a-courtin'!'

In the same village I heard of another example of country wit; but this one, I must confess, dates further back – to the days when farmers went about their job quite differently from the way they do to-day.

The custom on a certain farm (a common custom then) was for the stockman to come along to the farmhouse each morning to get the men's orders for the day. The farmer would still be abed, and the stockman, approaching under the bedroom window, would give first a modest little cough, than another and another, louder every time, to wake his master. But one winter morning the farmer woke in a bad temper. Truth to tell, he had been up very late the night before, celebrating with some of his cronies. 'Mornin', sir!' the stockman called up the bedroom window. 'What's the orders for to-day?' 'I don't know what you'd better do,' said the farmer, too sore about the head to be bothered with such matters at that early hour. 'Nor don't I, neither,' the stockman replies. 'Oh, go and hang yourself!' called the farmer. 'T'others too, sir?' asked the stockman, as he shuffled off out of the yard.

In fact, the countryman, for all he has been laughed at and gibed at so many years, is not nearly so dumb as the townsman may think him to be. And here is one last tale to prove it.

A very spick-and-span motorist once lost his way in the twisting lanes beyond the village. Signposts, when there were any, did not help him, because they only pointed to places he had never heard of and in any case did not wish to go to. At last he saw an old labourer coming along under the hedge, a sack on his back, and his pipe upside down in his mouth, for it was raining. The motorist asked him the way. For reply he received a long list of instructions that involved a sugarbeet field, a farm way back in the fields, a turn this way and a turn that way, a burnt-out oak tree, and various other landmarks which, though they were as familiar as his own hand to the old labourer, meant nothing whatever to the impatient motorist. Seeing he would never get any forwarder, the motorist lost his temper and called the old man a fool. 'I may be a fool,' was the slow response, 'but I ain't bliddy well lost!'

The Librarian

The other day the first tenants moved into the comfortable little flats that have been carved out of the old Gild Hall. The event was not without significance in the village story. But its immediate importance, of course, was for the tenants themselves, one of whom, indeed, had gone about in a dream for weeks, popping in and out with a tape measure to see if and where her furniture would fit, until it was almost feared for her health. She could hardly bring herself to believe it really was true that her application had been approved, so great was the contrast between the new flat and the old dreary cottage she had had to pay good rent for, though it leaked, lacked even the minimum convenience, and would soon have tumbled about her head.

Nor were the other tenants less happy – even the one who had had to make the momentous decision to part with her piano. 'I know I don't play it,' she said, 'but it did make such a lovely piece of furniture. The keys were solid ivory; and, well, you don't see many pianos about these days with solid ivory keys, do you?'

It was perhaps this obvious satisfaction of the tenants that, more than anything else, set the seal on a long and arduous effort on the part of certain members of the community to safeguard one of the village's most interesting old buildings and at the same time to make a modest contribution towards the solution of the housing problem.

Prior to its present transformation, the Gild Hall had posed rather a teaser to the local authorities. It is one of the oldest buildings in the parish, and its history (as much of it, anyhow, as the Parish Records can be made to reveal) throws a revealing light on certain aspects of village life in the past. It comprised a spacious upper room, known as the schoolroom; four pokey almshouses; a dim and draughty cubby-hole given over to the village library; and various nondescript oddments. But the whole building had been allowed to fall into such a state of disrepair that demolition was threatened.

Not that this seemed to perturb the majority of the village, if the many outspoken comments were to be taken at their face value. The younger generation in particular showed little concern for the fate of the old building. Such a ramshackle place, it was held, would be best out of the way, and some nice sensible dwelling-houses ought to be put up in its stead.

Superficially, there was a good deal to recommend this point of view. The Gild Hall was undeniably becoming an eye-sore, even a disgrace. It was dangerous. Its windows were half out, its walls crumbling. The only purpose it seemed to serve now was as a dark and dubious playground for some of the more harum-scarum village children. And yet, after all, it was the Gild Hall. And ought not its great age to count for something?

Qualified architects put the date of the Gild Hall as fifteenth century, with certain additions about a hundred years later. These additions were probably the four almshouses (predecessors of the present flats) and the schoolroom. The whole made a not unimposing pile, boasting a fine overhang, some magnificent Tudor chimneys, oak beams, and an unusual gateway entrance that opened right through the building into the churchyard. In this gateway there was a curious double hatch door where, even within living memory, bread was handed out for the relief of the poor in exchange for metal discs branded with the Guardians' stamp and the number of loaves to be collected. One way and another, the Gild Hall had been a focus of village life for centuries – not least, perhaps, the schoolroom part of it, which may originally have housed the Gild and which even now contained relics of its later use in the shape of elm-wood desks heavily scored with scholars' dates and initials. Incidentally, there is an entry in the Parish Records, for 1724, telling that Dan'l Wade the taylor was paid thirteen shillings 'for making blew gowns' which may well have been for the girls of the school.

As for the almshouses, these were bequeathed to the parish by the squire in 1630 and had been continuously occupied by village widows until the early years of the present century. Some of the very last of the widows are still remembered, including one who was extravagantly (and enigmatically) known as Lady Tealeaves. A relic of another of them survives to this day in the form of a bush of the old Maiden's Blush rose which not even the trampling and rough handling of the builders' men has been able to kill.

One of the chief objections to the almshouses, it soon transpired, was that they opened directly on to the churchyard (and turned their backs on the road). Many villagers, especially some of the older ones, have an ingrained horror of the idea of living cheek by jowl with the dead. Presumably, there is a fear of ghosts. 'I know I dussn't walk through the old chu'chyard at night,' said one of them; while another was probably voicing a pretty general opinion when she said, 'I shouldn't think anybody would want to look out on their dear husband's grave every day, like that.' Can it be that we are more squeamish than our forebears were? Or is it simply that the widows who originally lived in the almshouses had no choice in the matter? Charity, we know, was not always a considerate hostess. The jakes, for example, lest it should offend the genteel on their way to church, was situated on the far side of the churchyard, a provision which may have been considerate for the worshippers but was hardly that for the old ladies directly concerned. Nor was there any water in the cottages, so that every drop had to be fetched from the village pump, when willing hands could be found to do so. There was not even an oven in the dark little rooms, and for their baking the almswomen were dependent upon the village baker.

As for the care of their health, this must have been a very chancy business. A Pest House (also called the Small Pox House) was situated on the outskirts of the parish and presumably took charge of the worst cases, while the local apothecary looked after the others. There is an item in the Parish Records for 1747 setting forth that this same apothecary, one Thomas Doughty, together with a 'surgeon' from the next village, agreed for £10 a year to 'look after and undertake to cure all poor persons of the parish who are not able to pay for themselves . . . in all branches of physic and surgery, in all the several distempers and ailments incident to human bodies, as sickness, lameness, broken bones, cutting off of limbs, smallpox, midwifery and all other illnesses whatsoever'. Another entry, concerning an actual case, is even more to the point. 'It is agreed between the inhabitants of the parish and

William Hazelfoot that he shall with the wife of Mr Griffeth cut off the leg of Thos. Wall for the sum of four pounds and to heal the stump and likewise other sores that are upon him.'

Villages are usually strong in inherited memory, and it may be that at least some of the antagonism to the proposed restoration of the Gild Hall came from the testimony the almshouses provided of the stern conditions of earlier times. Happily, however, there was a hard core of more objectively minded parishioners who determined that, come what may, the venture should go through. Accordingly, a body of Trustees was set up and the complicated task was begun of sorting out the muddle of the various charities involved and of finding the considerable sum of money needed not only for the restoration and safeguarding of the general structure but also for the conversion of the four almshouses into self-contained flats. Looking back, now that the experiment has proved itself, one wonders how on earth it was done. As so often happens in such cases, the final successful outcome was due in no small measure to the single-minded perseverance of one person, whose insistence and drive allowed no obstacle to remain in the way.

Every possible source of income had to be exploited. Public bodies were approached for contributions; likely Trusts were written to again and again; a Friends of the Gild Hall society was organized; private loans were invited; fairs and exhibitions were held; collecting boxes were put at points of vantage; and even a dingy assortment of Roman shards and coins, dug up in the locality, was sold off to happy visitors at a penny a piece. In short, the art of wheedling was so successfully employed that presently sufficient money was assured to justify setting the builders to work. And so, under the scornful gaze of the critics, the scaffold-poles were set up and it became generally realized that the restoration of the Gild Hall was indeed to become a fact.

But it was a long job and not without its moments of intense anxiety, as when, for instance, prospective benefactors shied off at the last minute or the original estimates had to be stepped up because of newly discovered structural weaknesses. However, the over-all reconditioning was at length completed and it was now possible to see what a fine old edifice had been saved from destruction. Not that the critics appeared impressed. When a well-known actress was asked to come along and declare the building open, which she did in a pretty speech, only a handful of people turned up, as if thereby, whether intentionally or not, underlining the general lack of enthusiasm for the whole affair.

The tide of adverse opinion did not turn, in fact, until, after yet more delays and hopes deferred, the flats themselves were finished and ready for occupation. Additional windows had been put in, admitting sun both morning and evening. The oak beams had been carefully cleaned and treated for woodworm. Every reasonable convenience for old people seemed to have been thought of. Even the colour schemes were bright and unconventional.

It was announced that applications for the tenancies could now be considered. The rents were to be five shillings a week. The only stipulations were that tenants must be women not in receipt of National Assistance and that dogs were not allowed – though other pets might be kept. Only the no-dogs clause produced any hesitancy. As one disappointed tenant said: 'I'd rather have a barking dog than an old budgerigar twitterin' all day long, anyhow!'

The face-about was now complete. Unabashed, the former critics joined in the general chorus of praise and approval. When the first lucky tenants moved in, their excited happiness almost provoked envy among the ineligibles. 'I'd love one,' somebody was heard to say; 'but there, it's no use: I've still got my old man.' Another said, 'I'd put my name down at once – if it weren't for my little bit of garden. I know I can't look after it, like my husband used to – he wouldn't have a weed on the place. All the same, no, I couldn't do without my garden.' As for the eligible tenants, no sooner were they installed when they found themselves the recipients of all sorts of unexpected visits. Not that they did not enjoy, and very much so, showing their visitors round. From these chatty tours of inspection nothing was omitted, whether it was the window-seat with a view up the street ('My friends like to sit here and have a cup of tea with me') or the shining bath and sink unit.

And so the Battle of the Gild Hall has been won. Loans have all been repaid. The balance sheet shows a tiny credit. An unsightly corner of the village has been transformed into a considerable architectural attraction. And, not least, a small but gratifying contribution has been made towards solving the housing difficulties of some of the older people. Their pleasure, now, is plain to see. If they have a complaint at all (and it scarcely merits the word) it is that there is still a regrettable tendency in the village to refer to their nice new flats as 'the almshouses' (so reluctantly does habit die) and that certain well-intentioned callers are still inclined to present themselves at the door rather in the manner of someone bringing the expected basin of charity soup.

Saturday afternoon is familiarly known as 'Library afternoon', this being the day, from two o'clock until four, when the Librarian is in attendance at the Gild Hall in the little room allocated for her use. The village is not only proud of its Library to-day, it is even fond of it. Indeed, it is almost as much a club as it is a library: gossip is exchanged there quite as much as books. At all times it radiates good cheer.

This was not always so. When the Library was first housed there, in the Gild Hall's derelict days, a drearier place for the dissemination of culture could hardly have been chosen. But then, of course, nobody attached any importance to culture, and the Gild Hall, being unsuitable for anything else and free for the asking, was voted to be 'just the very place'. Looking back on those not so very distant days, one marvels that anybody was found hardy and devoted enough to tackle the job of Librarian under such circumstances. The room was unheated, the windows were full of holes, and, for lack of shelves, most of the books had to be dumped on the floor.

But now that the Gild Hall has been reconditioned, all this is changed. The Library is as comfortable as anybody could possibly wish. Oak shelves have been fitted in; a Whist Drive was organized to buy an electric fire; the Librarian herself provided cheerful curtains; and a modest income has been secured from a charity bequest made over two hundred years ago by Ann Cole for the purpose of 'promoting the education of the people of the village'. Efficient as the Library is nowadays, it nevertheless manages to retain an easy, rural atmosphere, and only a regulation plaque over the door reminds members that, although it is a voluntary affair, it is also in effect a branch of the County Library itself, whose Chief Librarian keeps a kindly and fatherly eye on the whole concern.

There is a stock of eight hundred books – rather less than one per head of the entire population. Half of these books are renewed every three months when a fresh stock arrives from the County Library. Each member is allowed two books a week, one of which is supposed to be non-fiction, though this rule is not enforced. Nor are there fines for defaulters, who are encouraged, instead, to put something in 'the Box'.

In other words, the Library enjoys the advantages, without suffering the penalties, of official protection. But then it is doubtful whether the project would have worked any other way, since the village naturally prefers the personal approach to everything, culture included.

Fortunately, this is well understood by the Librarian. She is certainly as knowledgeable in the matter of books as anybody in the village; but even more to the point, perhaps, is the fact that she is no less knowledgeable of the preferences, not to say foibles, of the Library's members. She knows exactly what Mrs Fisher means, for instance, when, scanning the titles of the more romantic brand of novels, she says she is looking for something that will ensure her 'a nice read' over the weekend. Similarly, when Mrs Green arrives, confused and flustered as ever, the Librarian at once comes to her aid with 'A little light love, Mrs Green? I've got just the thing for you this week.' And if Mrs Podgers, feeling unequal to the trudge up the hill, should send Mr Podgers along instead, his shyly mumbled request ('Mother sayd, *you* choose her something, please') will receive just as careful attention as if it had come from a more sophisticated reader.

Incidentally, the arrival of any man on the scene is apt to cause a flutter among the congregated members. If it is merely Mr Pierce, of course, whom everybody is on easy terms with, he will have to endure no more than the usual good-natured badinage; but if he should hail from the loftier hierarchies his entrance will freeze the ladies into an immediate silence, during which eyes peer stealthily over the tops of glasses or pore abstractedly on hurriedly turned pages; and not until he has gone and is well out of the way will the silence breathe again into whispered comments and subdued criticism.

Since the Gild Hall faces directly on to the churchyard, so, too, of course, does the Library. Such an arrangement, it might be thought, would be conducive to that peace and quiet which is properly associated with books. And so it is; but this is not the reason why the members themselves agree as to its suitability. More pertinent, so far as they are concerned, is the fact that it assures the best possible view of weddings and funerals. On such occasions, therefore, the Librarian sensibly acknowledges the prior claim of real-life drama over its fictional counterpart and temporarily abdicates. There is little else, indeed, that she could do.

If it should be a funeral that causes the interruption, members will crowd round door and window, silently respectful or tearfully reminiscent, waiting for the moment when, the mourners having at last departed, they can pop across to the grave and examine (not without silent comment) the size and quality of the floral tributes and the wording of the accompanying inscriptions. If, on the other hand, the occasion should be a wedding (and most village weddings seem to take place on Saturday afternoons) there is virtually no Library at all until the bridal party has left the church and gone down to the Village Hall for the reception; and then there is a sudden scramble back to the Library of members so voluble and bewildered that their book-choosing goes all to pieces and even the Librarian's entries are inclined to get out of hand.

Otherwise, 'Library afternoon' usually runs more or less true to pattern. Invariably among the first to arrive is Mrs Trail. She likes to select her books (two for herself, and two, but only in name, for Albie, her husband) quietly and at leisure, reserving her cheerful chatter for later, when her own choice has been made and others are trying to make theirs. Albie's share in the weekly orgy of fiction would seem to be confined to those tit-bits which she reads aloud to him as he sits dozing and smoking by the fire. His usual comment, according to Mrs Trail, is simply, 'The stuff you do bring into this house, woman!'

Presently Mrs Duffy comes bustling in. Her diminutive figure is almost smothered in books, armfuls of them, for she undertakes the onerous task of acting as weekly book-carrier and exchanger for several of her less able (or less willing) neighbours. She is, and needs to be, very systematic – though it is a system only she herself can recognize – and appears to be most intimately familiar with the literary likes and dislikes of her clientele. Having tucked each ticket into its appropriate book, she arranges her precarious burden, and, with a last laughing word to everybody, departs – but not before she has dropped a coin into 'the Box' by way of thank-offering, modestly remarking, as she does so, 'They say every little helps.' It is the Librarian's constant hope, by the way, that others will take example from Mrs Duffy's ill-afforded generosity; but it has to be confessed that for the most part the hint is not taken.

Mostly, those who attend the Library are women, not so much because the men of the village do not read as because their Saturday afternoons are usually otherwise occupied. Possibly, too, they include Library attendance among the strictly feminine jobs, such as flower-gardening, cooking, and washing-up, in none of which would they dream of lending a hand.

As to the kind of books preferred, Fiction, of course, is an easy first, with Biography and Travel next in favour. Only very occasionally is there a request for anything at all unusual – the few discriminating readers in the village being a category of their own and inclined to order their books direct by post from the County Library. The one sort of books for which, rather surprisingly, there is almost no demand at all is country books, the assumption being, presumably, that it would be a waste of time to read about something that is already familiar.

If country books are asked for, it invariably turns out that the request comes from some townswoman who has come to live in the village. There was the case of Mrs Drage, for instance. For her, the move from town to country has proved an adventure, a constant source of discovery. Even in looks she has changed, her pale cheeks having won a healthy colour and her step a lightness. 'Have you anything about birds?' she asked the startled Librarian one day. And from the chats that followed this unusual request, it appeared that Mrs Drage had turned into a great walker and that her chief delight now was the birds she never tired of watching. Even the sparrows that nest in her thatch are a joy to her. 'Look!' she says to her husband as she watches the sparrows dust-bathing in the path. 'What are they?' He, coming from country stock, smiles and says, 'Well, *we* used to call 'em dirty little birds!' Recently, she arrived at the Library agog with the information that she had been watching a kingfisher as she was leaning over the bridge. 'My husband says it's rare,' she announced, excitedly. 'Is it, really?' Rare or not, it had roused her heart like a poem: she had not guessed there were such beautiful birds uncaged and on the wing for every countryman to enjoy.

As four o'clock draws nearer, the arrivals become less and less frequent, until the last member of all has departed, having bundled her books into the shopping-bag along with the groceries and such gifts of fruit and flowers and vegetables as she may have picked up on the way. Then the Librarian herself turns out the fire, draws the curtains, and goes home. One more 'Library afternoon' has run its course, leaving everybody the richer not only by reason of the books they have borrowed but also by the social occasion for which these have provided the excuse. Surely Ann Cole would be more than satisfied to see how her good deed still prospers after all these years? Whether she would consider that the education of the village had thereby been properly 'promoted' is another matter.

Up with the Lark

It is one thing to enthuse over the the dawn chorus of the birds at this time of the year, and quite another to get up at three-thirty in the morning to hear it. Unless, of course, you happen to be a professional bird-watcher, one of that gallant band who think nothing of squatting for hours in damp ditches and would as soon be out of their bed as in it. All that most people hear of the dawn chorus, however eloquent they wax about it, is what comes in at the open bedroom window when they happen to wake one morning a lot earlier than usual. But that is not at all the same thing as hearing it out in the fields – not at all, believe me; and I am in a position to be emphatic on this point, because, much as I like my bed, I *have* risen at three-thirty to hear the birds, and I recommend it as an experience which everybody should enjoy at least once in a lifetime.

I ought perhaps to explain that it is not quite so difficult for me to go out into the fields at that unearthly hour as it would be for some people, for my cottage is practically surrounded by fields. All I have to do is to go through the gap in the hedge at the bottom of the garden. And I need not worry about being watched. There *are* a few other cottages in the lane close to mine, but their kindly inhabitants have long ago ceased to be astonished at my goings-on; and besides, at that hour, like most sensible citizens, they are fast asleep.

So it was that at what seemed like zero hour I pulled myself out of bed, dressed, made myself a quick cup of tea, and scrambled through the hedge into the fields, picking my way by the aid of a torch. For although by then it was ten minutes to four it was still dark, or at least not light enough to extinguish the major stars. And for the next five minutes, as I stood there waiting in the wheat, there was absolute silence: I seemed to be the only person in the world. Then, from some way off, I became aware of a skylark singing, so faint that I could scarcely hear it; but it was a signal that others must have heard plainly enough, for almost immediately there were skylarks singing every-where: the dark was suddenly full of lark-song and nothing *but* lark-song. Despite the quantity of it, it was a fragile song, the first small voice of the morning that was just being born. It was now four o'clock, and for five minutes the larks had it all to themselves – larks, and ever more larks, singing, sure enough, 'at heaven's gate' but long before 'Phoebus 'gins arise'. I think those five minutes, with only the skylarks singing and a few stars still faintly shining, were the most magical moment of the whole dawn chorus. Even at the time I felt that nothing I might hear presently, when all the other birds woke up and sang, could possibly be as beautiful as this ecstatic song at the peep of dawn.

To get a better view of the growing light, I moved across the fields into the open. Over in some shadowy elms on the horizon I noticed a spark of golden light. Presently it sailed clear of the trees and I saw that it was the moon – the old moon, with only two more days to run – 'the fringe of a finger-nail held to a candle', as Gerard Manley Hopkins says. As it climbed still higher, into the clearer air, it changed from gold to silver, and would vanish altogether when the morning light had grown stronger.

In fact, colour was beginning to assert itself, but still very tentatively, so that the wheat leaves were grey, as if covered with dew, and the hawthorn in the hedges and the sheep's parsley in the ditches had the ghostly whiteness of flowers seen by moonlight.

Absorbed in all this, I did not notice that the skylarks had stopped singing. Silence had returned – but not for long. At a quarter past four the rooks in the great rookery up at the Hall woke and began to squawk – hundreds of them greeting one another with a raucous 'Good-morning', as if they had not yet cleared their throats. I fancied too that somewhere I could hear a blackbird; but while I was straining my attention to make sure, a cuckoo called nearby – then another and another – until, from the four quarters, four cuckoos were challenging each other with tremendous and rather foolish emphasis.

Now it was the blackbirds' turn. They were soon at it in earnest. Near at hand, in what was still little better than half-light, I saw them fly out of the bushes and hedges where they had been roosting, silhouettes of birds, their spread wings suffused with morning light. Others – thrushes, too – were singing from the fieldside spinneys and distant woods; and their combined song was so strident, even shrill, that for a while I did not hear the smaller birds that had joined in, robins and finches, wrens and warblers, like a subdued harmony going on beneath the bold melody of the thrushes and blackbirds.

By four-thirty the chorus was at its best, or at any rate its loudest. The whole parish was full of bird-music, the air was thick with it. I should not have supposed there were so many birds in the fields and woods round my home; and if there were so many in these few square miles, what myriads there must be in the entire countryside – and all, at this moment, singing at the top of their voices.

While the chorus had been building up to its climax, colour too had been increasing in intensity – hue by gradual hue, unfolding slow as petals. And in the eastern sky, where the old moon was fast fading out of sight, there were wisps of pink and rose and green, so unblushingly sentimental that no painter would dare to put them on canvas. And it was all inextricably part of the experience of being out there in the fields listening to the dawn chorus of the birds, and I must stress, if I may, that this is not at all the same thing as lying abed and listening through the open window. Out there, my senses were stretched to their utmost, trying to cope with the sheer intensity and variety of it all, the song, the colour, the freshness and newness of the first of the morning.

And then, in another five minutes, the singing was all over. I had not expected it to end so abruptly. Suddenly I found myself standing in the silent fields again. Ordinariness had come back to the world. Well, nature is a past-master at achieving effects, and I expect this was the right way to end such a superb concert, with no encores to spoil it – only silence and the memory of what had been.

Even in the daytime we marvel at the song of the May birds; but what we hear then is no more than a hint of the dawn chorus itself. One almost wonders, afterwards, if perhaps one did not dream it. For how could there possibly be such a jungle-riot of bird-song, every dawn for the best part of a month, and nobody – or almost nobody – bother to get out of bed to hear it? Still, for all my enthusiasm at this moment, I expect I shall stay in bed tomorrow morning, and all the other mornings, like everybody else.

I pushed my way through the hedge and came indoors, first taking a glance at the other cottages in the lane. No smoke curled up from their chimneys, the windows were still shut, no dog barked to be let out of its kennel. It would be a full hour yet before Fred and Charley and the rest of them came stumbling downstairs to a breakfast of fried onions and then went off to another day's work on the farm. Farm-hands, no more than the rest of us, do not these days get up with the lark.

Promise of Spring

One of the things I always used to look forward to, when I was a boy, was the day in early spring when the gypsies would come to the door with hanging baskets of primroses for sale. These baskets were made of unpeeled hazel wands, tacked together criss-cross, and lined with moss in which whole roots of primroses had been 'planted' with charming effect. In short, I thought them the best value money could ever hope to buy.

I don't know which fascinated me more, the gypsy women, with their shiny black hair (I was told they greased it with hedgehog fat) and their soft wheedling voices and their babies asleep in carpet hammocks slung over their shoulders, or the primrose baskets themselves, smelling of damp earth and moss and the open air. 'You shouldn't encourage the didicoys,' my father would say: 'they're a lot of thieves. Why, they'd steal the skin off your back while you weren't looking.' All the same, it would have been unthinkable to let such things prevent us from buying one of their baskets to hang between the lace curtains in the window. It seemed to bring the woods into the house.

Of course we could have gone to the woods ourselves and brought home our own primroses — we often did so — for we lived deep in the primrose country, where they grew in every copse and spinney and spilled out on to the grassy banks beside the lanes; but that would not have been at all the same thing. Besides, the gypsies always seemed to be able to find primroses earlier than anybody else, as if they knew the secrets of the woods better. And in any case I am sure we could not have made such natty baskets as they did, with their nimble fingers. Perhaps I liked those primrose baskets as much for the sake of the gypsies who sold them as I did for themselves.

Later, however, I came to like primroses in their own right; better, in fact, than any other wild flower. And I still do. With their fragrance and candour and promise of spring, they seem to me the perfect flower. They are as frank and simple as Purcell's music – and as English. For, although they grow almost anywhere, not only in these islands but in all the temperate countries of Europe, there is nevertheless something essentially English about them, or so I like to fancy.

It is the more ironical, therefore, that for some years now I have chosen to live in one of the few parts of England where (at any rate in the immediate vicinity) there are no primroses growing wild. They do not seem to like the boulder clay, with a good deal of lime in it, of which our soil consists. Instead of primroses we have oxlips, which, although they are members of the same family, are quite different in habit and colour and leaf and even smell. Oxlips do not grow singly, as primroses do, but in bunches, anything from three or four up to thirty and more on a single head; and they are buff-yellow; and their leaves are less crimped than the primrose's.

Our woods are full of oxlips and lovely they look with the spring sunshine filtering down on them through the bare boughs. The village children gather them by the armful (for their stalks are long) and while the season lasts you may see jam-jars filled with them in cottage windows and sometimes a home-made notice tied on to the gate 'Oxlips, 3d a bunch'.

To somebody like myself, however, born and brought up in primrose country, oxlips can never be more than a very good second-best. And so each spring – or even a little earlier, when the bowling white clouds promise hail and the blackthorn is still in bloom – I go on a pilgrimage to some primrose woods I know in another part of the county. For there is nothing like primroses to set the seal, as it were, on the promise that in spite of bitter winds and laggard buds the wonder season of the year will soon be here. They gladden the child in all of us – and the poet in us, too.

I recall a March morning when I was walking through some recently cleared woods in Suffolk with a well-known writer. All about us the primroses flowered in great bosses and clumps of bloom, more freely than I had seen them anywhere. After a while, I strayed off on my own, to see what the deeper woods might yield; and when I came back to the clearing I found my friend sitting on a hazel stool that was literally awash with a yellow tide of primroses. He was gazing down at them, so lost in his thoughts that he did not hear me approach; and so I turned back, unwilling to disturb him. I always like to think that I thereby saved a poem that might otherwise have been lost.

Certainly he was luckier in his enjoyment of those primroses than another friend of mine who actually owns a wood where they grow. There is nothing, among all his treasures, and he is a rich man, that he enjoys more than his wood when the floor of it is yellow with Easter's flower. Or, rather, there is nothing he would enjoy more if he were allowed to do so; for, although he owns the wood, others, it seems, get the joy of it. During the blossoming season people pour out of the nearby town and settle on the primroses like a flock of pigeons in a field of peas. My friend tried protecting them, but somehow it did not work, and he gave up. He even tried sarcasm. 'Look!' he said, strolling one day anonymously among the crowd of happy pickers and finally taking his stand beside a woman who was grabbing at the flowers for dear life, 'Look! there's one you've missed.'

In fact, just when he would most have enjoyed his primrose wood it was scarcely his any more. His dream of wandering solitarily among the flowers, while the birds sang overhead, remained only a dream. It would almost seem as if we are not meant to own anything so precious as a primrose wood.

Very likely it is better to enjoy other people's. And if we must have primroses of our own as well, there is always the garden, of course. They may not look quite so happy growing there, as they would in their natural habitat, for, when we come down to it, nature is always the best gardener. Still, they will look pretty enough.

We might even go in for a whole primrose garden, like one I have in mind in a quiet hamlet. It stands beside a brick-and-tile bungalow that would not otherwise invite a second glance. It belongs to an old widower, a countryman to the core of him, and, like all genuine countrymen, not afraid of simple sentiments. The primrose was always his wife's favourite flower; and after she died, he had the charming idea of making a primrose walk in the tiny spinney that ran beside his garden, as a memorial to her. He trod a zig-zag path under the trees, and planted primrose roots by the score on either hand. They thrived so well under his loving attention that in time the spinney was full of them: one could hardly pick a way down the path without treading on them.

Often, on a spring evening, I used to see him sauntering beneath the sun-dappled trees, his hands folded behind him, lost in meditation among the pale primroses growing all about him.

The 'Black Horses' at Plough

The last yellow leaves were spinning down from the trees as I climbed the hill to Thurstons. The afternoon was still and golden, the only sound was the mewling of a flock of peewits overhead, themselves like drifting leaves. Then I heard the distant toot of a steam whistle, short and sharp and rather absurd. That, I guessed, would be Mr Jackson's steam plough – something of a rarity these days, even an excitement. I hurried over the ridge to see.

And there they were, the two enormous black engines, twice the size of the usual traction engine, one on either side of the long, sloping field, with tall plumes of smoke rising from their wide-mouthed funnels. I could just make out the plough itself, riding low on the cable between them; but the misty air, suffused with sunlight, made a silhouette of everything; so I crossed the stubble fields for a nearer view.

On the first engine I found Eddie, Mr Jackson's son, in charge, and as I approached he waved his oil can and rag in greeting. I climbed on to the platform for a word with him. But conversation was not easy. He had to keep an eye on the further engine, ready for the moment when its driver, pulling on the reversing lever, set the flywheel running backwards, unwinding the cable from the drum for the plough to make its return journey. In fact, hardly had we begun talking when he stopped in mid-sentence, manipulated the levers, and the giant engine began throbbing and shaking beneath us.

Slowly the plough drew nearer, Mr Jackson at the steering wheel and one of the farm-hands sitting beside him. I watched its progress with fascination. A steam plough is really two ploughs, one on either side of a central axle, like the two halves of a see-saw: while one plough is working, the other is hoisted in the air, its six mould-boards glinting like silver sails.

As he came up to the engine, Mr Jackson called out, 'Do you want a ride? Hurry up!' I leapt off the engine, and hastened round to the plough as the two men were pulling on the suspended shares and mould-boards, easing them down to the ground. 'Take a pew,' said Mr Jackson, pointing to a stout plank that did service for a seat. I cocked a leg over the already straining cable, clambered aboard, and immediately we were on the move.

There is nothing in all the mechanized work of a modern farm, I think, to match the thrill of a ride on a steam plough, and it is something very few people have a chance to experience any more. For one thing, I was surprised at the silence, once the plough has drawn away from the engines: I even fancied I could hear the roll and plunge of the furrows turning close under me. As for the motion of the thing, perhaps Mr Jackson was a little prejudiced when he said 'It's a lot better, isn't it, than being jolted to a jelly on a tractor', but certainly it was quieter than I had expected.

But what fascinated me was the action of the six shares cleaving the ground so close beneath me, while the mould-boards heaved the gleaming clods up and over, great waves of earth rising, curling, crumbling into place. Looking down between the iron struts it was as if the solid ground had suddenly become fluid, rolling and churning as in the dawn of time.

This is ploughing almost on the prairie scale, six furrows at a time, and nine or ten inches deep. The rate is about an acre and a half per hour. 'Say what you like,' said Mr Jackson, 'you can't beat it, especially on this heavy land. It helps the draining. It ploughs *better*, for the simple reason that the additional speed (it runs at about six miles per hour) breaks up the land better, makes it more friable.' And certainly he can point to his excellent crops of corn and roots, year after year, as evidence.

Most farmers would probably protest that whatever the merits of the steam plough may have been in the past, it is now quite out of date and uneconomic – almost a museum piece, in fact. For one thing, it requires at least five men on the job – a man to each engine, two men on the plough, and another man to fetch and carry coal and water. The 'Black Horses', as these engines used to be called in the days when they were less unusual, are hungry and thirsty beasts. As Eddie was saying, when his duties stopped him in mid-sentence, 'I suppose we use anything from one and a half to two hundredweights of coal to the acre, especially now that steam coal is no longer available.' With fuel and labour the cost it is to-day, therefore, the outlay is heavy. Add to this the cost of the engines (which are not in production any more) and it will be seen that altogether steam ploughing is an expensive business.

But Mr Jackson took over the engines from his father when he took over the farm. Indeed they have been part and parcel of his working life ever since they first arrived at the farm, forty years ago, having cost his father then something over £5,000. By hiring them out to other farmers in the district the old man was able in time to get his capital back; but that could not happen to-day, for nobody wants them.

Perhaps, in the end, one of the reasons why Mr Jackson clings so tenaciously to his 'Black Horses' is because he really does enjoy ploughing with them. I think it might almost be said he is fond of them – a fondness due, no doubt, to association. When his father was still running the farm, in the years between the wars, one of Mr Jackson's jobs was to take the plough round the countryside, on hire for ploughing and draining, here, there and everywhere. Such work offered the young man a welcome release from the daily routine at home: it brought him into touch with all sorts of people and introduced him to varying ways of farming. It may have been hard and dirty work, and long hours into the bargain, but he recalls it with pleasure now and has many a laugh over some of the amusing incidents in which it involved him.

There was, for instance, his encounter with the irate colonel. He had left Thurstons at dawn with the first engine, the second to follow in due course. As he was passing the colonel's house, outside a neighbouring village, he had occasion to stop for a moment. He was just about to start up again when the colonel, dressed only in his pyjamas, rushed out of the gates and soundly berated him for making such a din outside his house so early in the morning. How, he demanded, was anybody to sleep with that infernal racket going on?

Mr Jackson proffered his apologies and the angry old man, presumably, went back to bed.

But a quarter of an hour or so later the second engine came along. Hearing this repetition of the 'infernal racket', and supposing, since the cause appeared to be identical, that Mr Jackson was playing a prank on him, the colonel once more rushed out into the road. His wrath this time was truly prodigious – and quite incomprehensible, of course, to the driver, who only learned what it was all about when he eventually caught up with Mr Jackson and swopped stories with him.

The mist was thickening as at last I made my way out to the road. I heard the steam whistle tooting its signal to call it a day. From invisible trees I could hear the chatter of innumerable starlings coming in to roost, and far off a pheasant called. Now, I thought, the men would be damping down the fires, and soon the two 'Black Horses' will be left to doze all night on the headlands, substantial ghosts from an earlier day.

Alpine Interlude

It is now four days since I arrived in Ehrwald. I had hoped to be in time to see at least the end of summer, instead of which I was in time to see what appeared to be the beginning of winter. Already, as the train climbed over the Arlberg Pass, I had had a foretaste of what I was in for. A blizzard piled the snow against the windows and shrouded the crocuses in the meadows. In the unheated carriage I buttoned my overcoat and shivered. And only the fact that I arrived in Ehrwald at night prevented me from seeing just how wintry a scene I had come to. A white morning, however, soon made it clear enough. That day, and the next, snow fell intermittently. The mountains that ringed the valley, when the low clouds let me see them, were capped with it. From the timber-line to far down the slopes, the forests of mingled larch and pine were sugared with it. Only on the floor of the valley did it melt almost as soon as it fell.

Such heavy falls of snow in September, I was told, were scarcely remembered even by the oldest inhabitants. Excited accounts were given of how the cows had had to be brought down for the Ehrwalder Alm a week or more before the traditional date. Nobody was prepared for such weather. Fearing that the cows would be cut off by the snow and suffer from the cold and lack of food, an emergency drive had been organized to bring them down, the whole community of peasant farmers uniting in an unusually cooperative effort forced upon them by the freakish weather. The boast now was that all the cows, numbering several hundreds and representing the best part of the wealth of the valley, had been brought down in record time and without a single casualty.

I had seen the cows being driven up to the Alm when I was here in

June, the gun-shot crack of the herd-boys' long, leather whips echoing through the forest. Even more would I have liked to see them being driven down again, for this event always constitutes something of an excitement. I could understand why everybody was so pleased that, despite the hazards, all the cows were now safe in their stalls. It is not only that they are the basis of the mountain farmer's economy. For the greater part of the year they share the same roof with him and his family, and how should he not feel a special, intimate concern for their welfare? Indeed, it is perhaps in part this intimate concern that impels him to decorate his cows with leaves and flowers, when, to the accompaniment of much shouting and horn-blowing and cracking of whips, they are brought down from the Alm. The incongruous garlands – branches of alpine roses and bunches of gentians slung round neck and horns – are, as it were, the farmer's way of expressing his joy and thankfulness that the cows' summer sojourn on the high Alm, fraught with real and constant danger, has been brought to a happy issue.

Until fairly recent years the decorations on such an occasion were much more elaborate – and still are so in some parts of the Tyrol. Special head-gear for the cows, composed of ingeniously made artificial flowers set in a huge shield, with perhaps an appropriate saint's picture in the middle, or a religious emblem, were fixed to the horns, flashing and flaming with colour, not unlike the tall head-dresses worn by masked men in the famous Tyrolean pre-Lent carnivals. These head-dresses were kept in the family from year to year, even from generation to generation. The cow-bells, too, were special to the occasion, larger than usual, flower-painted, and of great resonance, while the wide, cloth neck-bands from which they were suspended were embroidered with floral designs and suitable religious texts.

But getting their cows down from the Alm, this year, was not the farmers' only anxiety. The unexpected snow had been preceded by long spells of heavy rain, with the result that the second crop of hay (there are two hay harvests here every year) had hung about much too long. It was still waiting for the weather to dry it out when I arrived in Ehrwald. At three thousand feet, hay, apart from potatoes, is almost the only crop; and if this fails, everything fails. Even in the showeriest autumn, however, hay harvest presents no great difficulties. Slim wooden uprights, four or five feet high, with sometimes three and sometimes four cross-pieces set at right angles to each other, are stuck in the ground; and on to these the hay is loosely forked, so that the air is continually blowing through and drying it. But this year the hay was no sooner dry than it was wet again; and so the process had gone on, day after day, week after week, until now it looked as if it never would dry out fit for use. All over the valley the long lines of hay-crosses were hung with a grey, sodden mess that saddened the heart to see it.

The weather has cleared now and the days are as warm and golden now as they were cold and white when I arrived. Anything, the natives say, can happen at three thousand feet; and that's the way it seems to be. So shallow is the earth here, and so stony, that it rinses out in a matter of hours. From the valley meadows, and from all over the slopes, the hay carts come slowly in, drawn by cows and an occasional ox; and, remembering the wet rags of hay that hung from the crosses a few days ago, it is astonishing how salutary it now looks.

The valley is green again – if valley it can be called that is really a spacious stretch of grassland, reclaimed, nobody seems to know just when, from the wild moor. Even now, in spite of an efficient system of irrigation dykes and ditches, the moor prevails in places, so that thin rushes mix with the grasses, marsh flowers abound, and the black earth here and there gives beneath the foot like a sponge mat. Perhaps at one time the whole place was buried under water? And there are mornings, at this time of the year, when, flooded with milk-blue mist, it almost seems as if it had become a lake again. Then the meadows, with their innumerable little hay-huts, are completely hidden, and so are the three villages that guard the entrances through the mountains from the outside world. The valley is roughly triangular in shape, and these three villages, Ehrwald, Lermoos and Bieberwier, occupy the three corners, peering at each other across the intervening grassland, vying with one another in a (more or less) friendly rivalry.

It is easy enough to describe the lay-out of the scene, but how shall I describe the appeal of it, the disturbing beauty with which, at this time of the year and especially at sundown, it haunts the heart? I shall not even try, at this stage of my diary: rather, I shall content myself with recording the fact that, as I climbed the vivid, grassy slopes this evening, while the sun threw long shadows from the larches and the church bells clanged from their baroque steeples down in the valley, I had the feeling of having come home. This was the Ehrwald I had learned to like so well last summer, when I first saw it. This was the Ehrwald whose picture I had carried in my mind ever since, trusting, if sometimes with no apparent justification, that it would not be too long before I saw it again and over a longer stretch of time. (They say that one is either so little impressed by Ehrwald that one never wants to see it again, or so much impressed that, although one only intended to stay a little while, one ends by staying for ever.) And now, here I was, with the promise of a whole year in this Tyrolean valley before me: here, happily substituting the reality for the dream, was Ehrwald itself, glowing in the golden autumn sunshine, serene and secure in its enchanted circle of snow-capped mountains.

But Ehrwald was all flowers when I was here in June: the meadows were more flowers than grasses. Well, they are all gone now, scythed and dried and stored with the grass in those little log hay-huts scattered all over the level floor of the valley and up the steep slopes. And yet, no, not all of the flowers are gone. Perhaps, indeed, it is the autumn crocuses – the last incredible blossoming of the year – that have really brought Ehrwald alive for me to-day. In the meadows there are drifts of them, lilac swathes of fragile blossoms, so unsubstantial in the winy light of evening that they are only to be seen when looking at them one way, so evanescent, despite their multitudes, that they seem more like a vague, delicate brush of pale colour over the grass than flowers. And, coming closer, how frail they are, as if, in her anxiety to bring them to bloom before the growing-time is over, nature has forced them overmuch, so that the stems, for lack of chlorophyll, are silky-white and of a substance so slight that they can hardly support the petals, which have fallen over, revealing, the better to aid the late-come bee, the close assembly of orange-coloured anthers. I do not know why D.H. Lawrence, in his exact and poetical descriptions of flowers, left the autumn crocus out of his bouquet: in its exposed nakedness, its seeming vulnerability, it is so completely his flower.

In the kitchen, this evening, I was showing some photographs of my Essex home, taken in spring, when the fruit trees were in bloom. Herr Sonnweber's favourite picture was one of an old apple-tree, its branches weighed down to the grass with flowers. In Ehrwald, any fruit tree is something of a rarity; and never in his life had he seen anything like this one. He was dazzled and could find no words. His wife, however, was more explicit. Displaying the photographs on the table, now this one and now that, 'You live in Paradise!' she said, sighing for envy. And when I told her I had thought it was she who had this extraordinary privilege, she dismissed my words with a sniff of contempt.

They've Started Harvesting

When the last sheaf of corn is being pitched on to the rick, the proper thing for somebody to say (at least in Essex) is: 'That's the one we've been looking for all harvest!' We all know it is going to be said, and we all smile when somebody says it – however often we may have heard it before. Without it, harvest would not be quite complete. It is a ritual. It says, in other words, that all has now been gathered in – the farming year has passed its peak – and now the men can ease up a bit. It is the farm-hand's 'Amen' to his thanksgiving for a safe harvest.

Of course there are other harvest rituals, too. Or rather, there were others before agriculture became a recognized industry and speed the first consideration. The internal-combustion engine, whatever else it may have done, has certainly knocked a lot of the fun out of farming. But some of the old harvest rituals still live on, in remote places, to remind us of a more leisurely age. I have seen men jump off the Last Load (tractor-drawn) and snatch a few green boughs from the hedge to take with them up to the stack-yard; and when the stack was finally topped off, those green boughs were fastened to the ridge, where they waved in the breeze till the thatcher came and pulled them down. Green boughs and singing always accompanied the Last Load in the old days; but the modern farm-hand doesn't sing at his work – I sometimes think he has forgotten how.

And he has forgotten how to make Corn Dollies, which were one of the best harvest rituals of all. But no, it isn't quite true to say he has forgotten this. In my own village, for example, and in several of the villages roundabout, there are still men who can – and do – make Corn Dollies; but they are all old men. The youngsters for the most part just look on and laugh. The skill and the poetry of these charming toys seem to mean nothing to them. Yet what lovely conceits they were! And what dexterity they showed in those knobbly old fingers, to be able to weave reluctant straw into such delicate shapes! Their original pattern was a sort of stylized female figure.

Indeed, antiquarians will tell you that they were probably intended as straw images of the goddess Demeter – pagan offerings fashioned out of the last sheaf of corn. However this may be, Corn Dollies were certainly a very old custom; and they were made not only in East Anglia but all over the country. They were taken to the farmer's house and hung up over the door. Or they were taken to the parish church and hung (as is still the case with us) among the roses and twining traveller's joy on the chancel screen.

Some of the Corn Dollies which are still made in my district, however, would hardly be recognized by Demeter. Anchors, aeroplanes, shepherds' crooks, ornamental tables, crowns, and even a set of fire-irons – these are some of the shapes I have seen, and as recently as last year. They were woven with just as much skill as the old traditional shapes; very delightful they looked, decked out with bows of red and blue braid and hung with barley tassels. The purist may frown on such departures from traditions; but I think the important thing is that Corn Dollies should still be made, of whatever shape. It is the skill that matters. And if the Essex farm-hand of to-day should prefer to model a straw aeroplane rather than a straw Demeter, well, what of it? He is far more familiar with aeroplanes, anyway, than with Roman goddesses.

Such harvest rituals and customs, of course, are all part and parcel of the excitement attendant upon the one supreme crop of the year. Corn is everything; and especially is this true in the Eastern Counties, where corn always has been, and still is, the basic crop. Every now and then there is talk of England ceasing to grow corn at all, because it can be so much more economically grown on the great prairies of the New World. But I think the Essex farm-hands would down tools if they were ever told that there was to be no more corn grown, but only cabbages and roots. Farming *is* corn-growing, to them.

The whole year leads up to harvest. As the summer advances, a crescendo of interest – even of excitement – mounts in the corn-belt villages. It begins in June. When we see the first wild roses blooming on the hedges, we say: 'Look! Eight weeks to harvest.' It goes on rising steadily throughout July, while the wheat turns from green to copper, as if it were accumulating the sunshine inside it, and the barley begins to hang down its head. And then, towards the end of the month, when you can hear the corn crackling in the noonday heat, the excitement becomes quite intense. Everybody talks corn, everybody thinks corn.

Down in the pub the men from the fields will be wearing out-size ears of wheat in their buttonholes, and all the old men's tales will be of summers long ago – of bumper harvests and lean harvests, of harvests that were taken in record time and of harvests that still lay out in the furrows when the first snow fell. And old women, who have scarcely set foot beyond their garden gates all through the year, will throw a shawl over their shoulders and hobble up the lane to see the ripening corn.

It is then, too, that you may see the farmer walking waist-deep through his wheat at evening. Every now and again he plucks an ear and rubs it in his hands and bites a milky kernel on his teeth. Carefully he reads the sky. Tomorrow, he decides, he will begin cutting.

But oh! that talk in the pub of harvests long ago. And of harvests not so long ago, too. For those days are still within living memory when corn was cut with scythe and sickle, and harvest was a feat of strength and a test of endurance. Many a man, long dead and gone, is remembered again every year for his skill with the scythe and for the number of pints of harvest beer he could drink in a day. The sheer physical labour of those men, their backs bent under the August sun, was surely incredible. 'And you'd hear them going home from the fields at night, singing' – so we are told; but what we are not told is whether it was from excess of vitality or from excess of beer.

Without a doubt, however, they were men of mettle; and it is not surprising that their memory now wears an aura. I shall never forget the scorn of one old man last year down in the village pub. Somebody was telling how two young boys – one aged twelve, the other eleven – had cut Farmer Ruffles's wheat for him because he was ill and his son had cracked a rib. One boy drove the tractor while the other rode the reaper. Everybody was full of admiration for them. But the old man took a long drink and slowly wiped the back of his hand across his lips. 'Well, of course,' he said at last, contempt in every word; 'it's *all* child's play nowadays!'

And so it would seem. The modern farm-hand rides across the field on his combine-harvester and the machine beneath him does all the work. No scything. No binding. No stooking. No carting. No stacking. No threshing. One minute the wheat stands upright in the field; and the next it comes trickling out of a funnel, clean grain ready for market. There was a good deal more to it than that in the old days. Men went in teams then, working across the field in echelon; and each team had its own 'Lordship' to lead the way and keep the pace and settle all disputes with the farmer. Farm work was collective and social; and that, perhaps, made all the difference. There was talk and there was fun. But now a man sits on his tractor and hears nothing but the chug of his motor from morn to night.

When the reapers had finished, and the last sheaves had been carted, the gates were opened to let the gleaners in. Like a flock of rooks they settled on the stubble, and were just about as noisy. They gathered the scattered corn into little nosegays tucked under the arm, and the shortheads they put into a 'titty bag' slung round the waist. They worked with great speed – till the gleaning bell from the parish church told them to stop. It was their aim to get enough corn to keep them in bread through the winter and so to save the rent. If the men sang going home at night, we are not told that the women did so too: for them another day's work waited in the house.

Well, it is all done with now, anyway. The only gleaning to-day is for back-yard hens. And the only time we hear the quiet hissing of a scythe in the corn is when some field has been so badly laid by wind and weather that the reaper-binder cannot get into it. But the old times live again, faint and dwindling, in the tap-room tales and in such ritual jokes as the one about the last sheaf. Or that other one about the leaning rick. When a corn-rick has been so clumsily made that it begins to fall to one side, needing support, the proper thing to say is: 'That's gone to Will's mother's!' Nobody knows (or cares) what it means.

Rhyme for a Farmer

Into his eager hand
Tumble the fruits of the earth.
It is his due, he says. At his command
Ten ears of wheat shall grow
Where there was one, and every field
Step up its yield
Without a pause for fallow. He buys
Power by the drum, fertility by the sack;
Farms to a blue-print. Wise
Beyond his fathers, he
Scoffs at their husbandry
Whose simple nostrum was
Force not the land.
Do the best a man may
(So they maintained)
There yet remained
A better to be done which would crown all.
But trust is a word not found to-day
In the farmers' dictionary.
Nor love. His heart is blind
Who sees no augury
In the small creatures under his charge
In hedge and ditch and verge,
And wryly smiles should he be told
That the last word
May yet be with the homeless bird
Driven before his stubble fires and the insect at bay
Drenched in the poison showered from his spray.

Epilogue

These words have been written to the accompaniment, on and oft, of the din of jet aeroplanes taking off from the nearby airfield whose runways are so placed that the planes are hurled immediately over my roof. This has been going on for years now and each year, with fresh improvements to the engines, the noise gets louder. Now and then a whole day goes by without a single plane taking off; and of course there are blessed days when fog blankets us and all planes are grounded anyway. But such periods of silence are the exceptions that prove the rule. For six months at one time, while the runways were being altered, there was complete silence and those months live in the memory still as a glimpse of paradise itself!

When the jets first arrived I wondered how I should endure the noise. Each plane that took off (and sometimes it would be a succession of planes, a dozen or more, one immediately after another) seemed to tear the sky asunder. A shiver ran through one's body from head to foot. Conversation was out of the question until the plane had passed from hearing. One used to begin a sentence, wait, begin again, wait again and finally give up with a shrug of despair. As for telephoning, this became an art of interpreting words that one had not heard. All this, I say, was how it was when the jets first arrived. But perhaps one really does grow an extra sense or perhaps it is simply because one cannot go on remonstrating against the inevitable. What cannot be improved must be endured. Anyway the noise is no longer quite so distressing as it was. One does not feel that if it goes on one day longer, one will go stark raving mad. One does not expect that just one more plane will suffice to split the ear-drums. One learns to wait until the immediate noise has died down without making facial gestures of despair. And when some caller, experiencing the din for the first time says, 'Does this happen often?' . . . one refrains from protesting that this particular exhibition is a very mild version indeed of what we are usually treated to – we know we should not be believed, anyway. Although one becomes more accustomed to the noise, however, it remains unpleasant. Was it for this that I sought out and came to the village of Finchingfield, considered to be one of the quietest places under the sun? Well we all ask ourselves that question but really, if it were not jets it would be something else. The world being what it is, and progress having taken the course it has taken, there is no escape. If we lack the resilience to adapt ourselves to the new conditions, then it is so much the worse for us. To be whole, we are told, everybody needs a drop of poison; and that must be our consolation.

Indeed, if one wished to give way to despair, there would be plenty of reasons for doing so quite apart from the nuisance of jet planes. It is twenty years since I came to Finchingfield and the changes that have taken place during that time amount to a revolution – in the people no less than in the place itself. But there is nothing new in this, unless it be perhaps that the changes occur more frequently now, more violently; but then the increased tempo of the times renders that inevitable. The point is that there have always been changes in the countryside; and those that occurred a hundred years or so ago were no less devastating at the time than those that occur to-day to us. John Clare is one of the most pertinent witnesses of this fact. As a young countryman, the son of a farm-labourer, in Northamptonshire in the early nineteenth century, he watched the loved and familiar contours of the land changed completely by the coming of Enclosure. And it was not only the landscape that changed – a new way of rural life was involved. But perhaps it was the spoilation of the countryside (as he saw it) that hurt him most – oak trees felled, baulks ploughed, bogs drained and all the minutely familiar scene changed utterly – he never ceased to grieve over it. Nor did the change of his little, so-loved world end with Enclosure. Returning from a walk one day in June 1825, he related that he had seen 'three fellows at the end of Royce Wood who I found were laying out the plan for an Iron Railway from Manchester to London.' So the Flying Scotsman today rattles over the ground where Clare saw the flowers grow and his private voice of protest was no more able to prevent its coming than we were here in Finchingfield able to stop them ploughing up Park Wood (famous for its oxlips) to build a runway. Moreover, such losses in the last twenty years have been more numerous than I could possibly reckon – of footpaths ploughed up during the war and never replaced, of fine old half-timber cottages pulled down for lack of the regulation cubic space of living room, of gracious mansions that embodied a complete culture, sold piecemeal to jobbers and dealers, of hedges bulldozed out of existence to enable a more economic working of the land, of trees felled by the hundred where every tree is as valuable ecologically as aesthetically, of Tudor pigeon-houses wantonly destroyed or allowed to fall to pieces, of cowslip meadows ploughed up and green bridle-paths choked out of existence – marvel is that so much of the old and wild still remains where development of the new and cultivated have had their way. I can still walk for miles without setting foot on a road or even a lane. For all the diminution of certain species of wild flower there are still enough remaining to make this little corner of English clayland arable, one of the most rewarding to flower-lovers in the country. Trees may be felled and not replaced, but there are still enough to cause a stranger to exclaim how fine our wild timber is – to provide shelter for as rich an assortment of certain classes of birds as any county can boast of. And, if architecturally we are a great deal poorer than we were even a few years ago, we are still rich enough to attract the curious visitor from far and wide.

Bibliography

This lists, in date of publication order, every book written by, compiled or edited by, or contributed to by C. Henry Warren. Reprints and American editions are not included, only new editions with additional material or by a different publisher or with a different illustrator. Although Henry Warren contributed many hundreds of periodical articles and poems, the best of his work was included in his books.

Pipes of Pan. Poems From Egypt. Collection of poetry. Erskine Macdonald, 1918.

A Book of Verse for Boys. Edited with Occasional Notes. An anthology of poems for secondary school pupils. Grant Richards, 1924.

The Stricken Peasant and Other Poems. Collection of poetry. Selwyn and Blount, 1924.

Cobbler, Cobbler and Other Stories. Collection of short stories and sketches. Faber and Gwyer, 1925.

'While 'Zekiel Ploughed'. Short story in *Best Short Stories of 1925*. Cape/Houghton, 1926.

Wild Goose Chase. Being the Journal of an Intimate Adventure into the New World. Journal of an attempt to emigrate to Canada. Faber and Gwyer, 1927.

The Secret Meadow and Other Poems. Collection of poetry. Faber and Gwyer, 1928.

The Men Behind the Music. Biographies of composers – including Handel and Mussorgsky by C. Henry Warren. Edited. Routledge, 1931.

Orchards of the Sun. A novel of Provence. Lovat Dickson, 1934.

Beside Still Waters. A novel of East Anglia. Thomas Nelson, 1935.

'Sir Philip Sidney' in *Great Tudors*, edited by K. Garvin. Essay about the life of Sir Philip Sidney. Nicholson and Watson, 1935.

The Writer's Art. A guide to writing. George Newnes, 1935.

The Beacon and Seven Other Poems. Collection of poetry. Privately Published, 1936.

A Cotswold Year. Journal of a year in the Cotswolds, illustrated by Bernard Hailstone. Geoffrey Bles, 1936.

Sir Philip Sidney: A Study in Conflict. Biography of Sir Philip Sidney. Thomas Nelson, 1936.

Wise Reading. A guide to reading. George Newnes, 1936.

A Boy in Kent. Childhood autobiography – Mereworth, Kent, endpaper drawing by Frank Kendon. Geoffrey Bles, 1937.

West Country. Somerset, Devon and Cornwall. A guide book – Somerset, Devon and Cornwall, illustrated with photographs. Batsford, 1938.

Happy Countryman. Biography of Freddie Dare, countryman of Finchingfield, Essex. Geoffrey Bles, 1939.

'Valleys and Orchards' in *The English Countryside*. Countryside essay on Kent. Batsford, 1939.

Corn Country. Textbook on corn-based agriculture of East Anglia, illustrated with photographs, paintings and prints. Batsford, 1940.

England is a Village. Countryside essays – Finchingfield, Essex – the Second World War, illustrated by Denys Watkins Pitchford. Eyre and Spottiswoode, 1940.

'Corn' in *England and the Farmer*, edited by H.J. Massingham. Essay about corn-based agriculture. Batsford, 1941.

A Boy in Kent. Childhood autobiography – Mereworth, Kent, illustrated by Charles Stewart. Hollis and Carter, 1942.

The Land is Yours. Countryside essays – Finchingfield, Essex, drawings by Thomas Hennell. Eyre and Spottiswoode, 1943.

Miles From Anywhere. Countryside essays – Finchingfield, Essex, drawings by Thomas Hennell. Eyre and Spottiswoode, 1944.

The Good Life: An anthology of the life and work of the countryside in poetry and prose. Edited, drawings by Alexander Walker. Eyre and Spottiswoode, 1946.

Happy Countryman. Biography of Freddie Dare, countryman of Finchingfield, Essex, illustrated by C.F. Tunnicliffe. Eyre and Spottiswoode, 1946.

Adam was a Ploughman. Countryside essays – Finchingfield, Essex, illustrated by John Aldridge. Eyre and Spottiswoode, 1947.

English Cottages and Farm-Houses. Textbook about English rural architecture, illustrated with colour plates and black and white drawings. Collins, 1948.

'Introduction' to *Bevis* by Richard Jefferies. Edited. Eyre and Spottiswoode, 1948.

'Introduction' to *A Gamekeeper at Home* by Richard Jefferies. Edited. Eyre and Spottiswoode, 1948.

'Introduction' to *Hodge and His Masters* by Richard Jefferies. Edited. Eyre and Spottiswoode, 1948.

'Introduction' to *The Open Air* by Richard Jefferies. Edited. Eyre and Spottiswoode, 1948.

'Introduction' to *Round About A Great Estate/Red Deer* by Richard Jefferies. Edited. Eyre and Spottiswoode, 1948.

'Introduction' to *Story of my Heart* by Richard Jefferies. Edited. Eyre and Spottiswoode, 1948.

Footpath Through the Farm, being a Simple Narration of the Practices and Purposes of Agriculture Throughout the Year. Textbook about farming, illustrated with black and white photographs. Falcon, 1949.

Essex: the County Book. Guide to Essex, illustrated and with a map. Robert Hale, 1950.

'Introduction' to *Essex, the Little Guide* by J. Charles Cox. Guidebook – Essex. Edited and revised. Methuen, 1952.

The Scythe in the Apple Tree. Countryside essays – Finchingfield, Essex, with photographs by Bertl Gaye. Robert Hale, 1953.

Tyrolean Journal. Journal of a Year in the Austrian Tyrol, with photographs by Klaus Hedbabny and the Author. Robert Hale, 1954.

'The Country comes to Town' in *Radio Times Annual*. Essay about the contrast between town and country. BBC, 1956.

Great Men of Essex. Biographical essays on famous Essex people (for children), illustrated with a map and seven half-tone plates. Bodley Head, 1956.

Autobiography (Piano in the Front Room/The Church on the Hill/ Content with What I Have). Unpublished autobiography – 1907 to 1937. 1957.

'The Cottage Garden' in *A Book of Gardens*. Study of cottage gardens. Cassell, 1963.

Countryman into Poet. BBC broadcast talk about C. Henry Warren's poetry with readings from *The Thorn Tree*. 1963.

The Thorn Tree: Poems. Collection of poetry. Dolphin, 1963.

Content with What I Have. Countryside essays – Finchingfield, Essex, illustrated by Susannah Holden, introduction by Richard Church. Geoffrey Bles, 1967.

'Why I Like Essex' in *Best of Essex Countryside* by E.V. Scott. Essay. County Guide Publications, 1976.

England is a Village. Countryside essays – Finchingfield, Essex – Second World War, illustrated by Denys Watkins Pitchford. Ashgrove, 1983.

A Boy in Kent. Childhood autobiography – Mereworth, Kent, illustrated by Charles Stewart, introduction by Geoffrey R. Warren. Alan Sutton, 1984.

BIBLIOGRAPHY

A Cotswold Year. Journal of a year in the Cotswolds, paintings by Raymond Booth, illustrated with contemporary photographs. Alan Sutton, 1985.